# Contents

FOREWORD ...................................

INTRODUCTION............................

1 - UNDERSTANDING PERSONALITY STYLES .................................................. 10

2 - THE IMPORTANCE OF VERSATILITY ......................................................... 13

3 - THE FOUR PERSONALITY STYLES – AN OVERVIEW ................................... 19
The Personality Grid.................................................................................................. 21

4 - THE FOUR PERSONALITY STYLES – IN DETAIL ........................................... 22
The Analytical personality......................................................................................... 22
The Driver personality............................................................................................... 23
The Amiable personality ........................................................................................... 25
The Expressive personality........................................................................................ 27
Shorthand description of the basic styles.................................................................. 30

5 - IDENTIFYING CUSTOMER STYLES ............................................................. 31
Identifying Analytical customers............................................................................... 32
Identifying Driver customers..................................................................................... 33
Identifying Amiable customers.................................................................................. 34
Identifying Expressive customers.............................................................................. 35

6 - IDENTIFYING YOUR BASIC STYLE .............................................................. 39
Personality Style Grid................................................................................................ 43
Plotting your personality style ................................................................................... 46

7 - BASIC STYLES & SUB-STYLES .................................................................... 49
Personality Grid - Sub Styles..................................................................................... 49
See yourself as others see you ................................................................................... 50

8 - MODIFYING YOUR SELLING STYLE............................................................ 53
Basic desires & fears ................................................................................................. 58

9 - MODIFYING YOUR ANALYTICAL SELLING STYLE ........................................ 59
Selling to Driver customers ....................................................................................... 59
Selling to Amiable customers.................................................................................... 61
Selling to Expressive customers ................................................................................ 63
Selling to fellow Analytical customers ..................................................................... 66

10 - MODIFYING YOUR DRIVER SELLING STYLE ............................................. 69
Selling to Amiable customers.................................................................................... 69
Selling to Expressive customers ................................................................................ 72
Selling to Analytical customers................................................................................. 74

Selling to fellow Driver customers ................................................................................ 77

## 11 - MODIFYING YOUR AMIABLE SELLING STYLE ................................................ 79
Selling to Expressive customers ...................................................................... 79
Selling to Analytical customers ....................................................................... 81
Selling to Driver customers ............................................................................. 83
Selling to fellow Amiable customers ............................................................... 86

## 12 - MODIFYING YOUR EXPRESSIVE SELLING STYLE ............................................ 88
Selling to Analytical customers ....................................................................... 88
Selling to Driver customers ............................................................................. 90
Selling to Amiable customers .......................................................................... 92
Selling to fellow Expressive customers ........................................................... 95

## 13 - CONCLUDING COMMENTS ................................................................................ 98

# Foreword

I became involved in direct selling in 1986, and in 1992 I read Steve Deery's books on prospecting. What I learnt from them made a significant contribution to the very successful network marketing business that I built up with my wife for the next eight years. I was therefore delighted to be asked to write the foreword for Steve's new book, 'How Customers Think: Or, How Customers Like to Buy '.

Within this book is the most comprehensive examination of buying and selling styles that you are ever likely to find. Steve delves deep into the four main personality styles, describing their mannerisms, vices, virtues and temptations. Readers will be left in no doubt about their own style. Customer buying styles are then explored in detail before an examination of how each selling style can and should be modified in order to sell more successfully to each type of buyer. The whole process is fascinating!

When I started selling, my main concern was what my potential customers thought of me. Much later I realised that finding out about them and how they liked to be treated was far more important, and made for improved results. If I had read this book 15 years ago I would have been more successful, sooner.

As Steve states, versatility is the key to success in selling. This book will help you to become an expert in assessing how your potential customers like to buy and altering your approach so that you can become more effective. It will also teach you a few things about yourself that you might not have known - which is always useful!

Peter Clothier 2013

Peter Clothier is the author of 'Multi-Level Marketing: A Practical Guide' (3rd ed. 1997, Kogan Page) and 'Network Marketing - How To Make It Pay' (1996, Insight)

# Introduction

Why is it that some customers buy from us and others do not? I suppose there could be any number of reasons for this. Perhaps it was affordability, a lack of need, or maybe the product itself. But suppose we establish that cost was not an issue, that the customer had a need, and that our product would satisfy that need. Yet still we fail to sell to the customer, and let's be honest we have all had this experience, then what else could it be? Well I guess this leaves two possibilities. It's either us, or it's the customer. So which is it?

Well we could take the responsibility and put it down to a shortcoming we have in our sales skills. This might spur us on to enrol on a sales training programme that makes good this shortcoming. Yet even having successfully completed such a programme we might still find customers capable of buying from us, but who still don't. If so does this mean failing to sell to customers is their fault rather than ours? Well which ever it is, I will say which later; it is not a situation any self-respecting salesperson can allow to persist. To do so is to tolerate missed sales opportunities – situations where we do all the work but don't win the order.

Whether we are selling brushes door-to-door or executive jets there will of course always be a gap between those customers who can buy, and those who actually do. This is often referred to as a closing ratio. Expectations as to what this ratio should be will vary from industry to industry. Perhaps one-in-six is the expectation if you are selling brushes and one-in-three the expectation if you are selling executive jets, it doesn't really matter. What does matter is that while we are all capable of having a 'good run' it is unlikely that any salesperson will have a sustained closing ratio of one-in-one. Anyone who does is not a salesperson but an order taker - quite a different occupation altogether! If you are an order taker, then this book will be of no benefit to you, why would you need it? On the other hand, if you are in the real business of selling then this book will teach you two things. Why there is a gap between those customers who can buy, and those who actually do. Secondly, how we can close this gap.

Just in case you get the wrong idea, this book is not about 'closing the sale'. If it were it would only be concerned with the second of our two objectives. Don't get me wrong, sales need to be closed. But it is not the objective here to teach you a battery of closing techniques to help close the sale. Better if we can avoid such reliance altogether. So the book is not about 'closing'.

Having made clear what the book is not about, let me make plain what it does concern. The book addresses how customers think. Or put more directly, how customers like to buy! Now the expression 'how customers like to buy' might strike you as odd. This wouldn't surprise me. I've attended hundreds of sales training courses over the years and read countless books on the topic without ever once coming across the expression. But is it so odd?

Just think for a moment about how you like to buy and how your partner or spouse likes to buy. Are they the same? Leaving aside any supposed differences in gender buying habits a little reflection reveals that different types of people like to buy in different ways. Some of us like service, others not; some like to ask questions, some not; some like to ponder, others not. And these are just a few of the obvious differences in the ways we like to buy. If we buy differently, and we too are someone's customers, why should our customers be any different?

If there is a difference in the way we like to buy, and I will show that there is, how do we find out how a given customer likes to buy? Well it requires we 'know the customer'. Now this expression could mean anything depending on how it is being applied, but here its use is very specific. When I say 'know the customer' I am not referring to their likes and dislikes, their personal circumstances, their buying habits, and so on, all of which are important. Rather by this expression I mean 'know how the customer likes to buy'! So how do we do this? Well the aim of the book is to teach you how.

But simply knowing how a customer likes to buy is only half of what is required to make a sale. Why? Because how the customer likes to buy is not, necessarily, how we like to sell. When the two styles or approaches fail to coincide we have a problem - no sale. A problem reflected in a closing ratio that is often not all it could be. Let me give you a taste of what I mean by way of the tale about 'When Sally met Harry'

Sally is an auto trader, and Harry her potential customer. Now during her career Sally has demonstrated a level of sales competence and seems to possess what some might describe as the hallmark characteristics of a car salesperson. Most particularly, a love of cars, how they work, and what they do. She is technically competent and proud of her product knowledge, and why not? But will it be enough to persuade Harry, who is now entering the showroom, to buy:

The initial interaction between Sally and Harry goes well as Sally guides Harry toward those cars that meet his two basic needs, that of type and price - so far so good. So, Harry is now in a position to decide between those cars that meet his needs. Now this is not a difficult position to get too in the sales process. In fact Harry could quite probably have arrived at this point without Sally's help. He needed only to locate those cars meeting his needs, say affordable family saloons. Nonetheless, Harry is, so far, appreciative of Sally's assistance and comfortable with their interaction. But from this point onwards things do not go well and Harry subsequently leaves without buying, despite having been presented with cars that more than adequately satisfy his two basic needs.

So what went wrong? Well, Sally wonders this too, though not for long. Another potential buyer has wandered into the showroom and requires the benefit of her technical knowledge, or so Sally thinks. So let us look at an example of what Sally actually said and then briefly analysis what went wrong.

Having narrowed the choice to two possible cars Harry then asked Sally whether they were available in manual. Sally's response was to detail at length the various options for each model. "This one comes with three transmission choices, a refined five speed manual, a new hypertronic CVT automatic and a CVT M6 which incorporates a six …", and so on. All this technical wizardry is important of course as without it we merely have so many hunks of metal. However, Harry is none the wiser following Sally's response because he switched-off long before she had finished. While it is clear Harry didn't appreciate the nuances Sally was good enough to point out we might ask whether in fact he actually needed this information. Sally certainly felt so and therefore rattled-off her technical sales presentation without further thought – this is how she always sells.

Yet Harry didn't actually want or need to know the technical detail in order to make a decision to buy. You see Harry is not technically minded at all, but rather a pragmatic kind of man. Consequently, most of what Sally said so enthusiastically passed over Harry like so much water off a duck's back. Harry is the sort of person content to assume that manufactures have had the foresight to supply each car with a fuel tank and a brake pedal that works. So long as the car has these, along with a few other observable additions like an engine, four wheels, and so on this is pretty much all Harry needs to know technically. Quite frankly he doesn't care about what goes on underneath the hood. All Harry really wanted to know was whether or not Sally could supply a manual version of either model in the colour he liked, at a price he could afford.

If Sally had been less concerned with imparting her expertise and more concerned with Harry's priorities then she might have made the sale. Sally's failure, rather than Harry's failure to appreciate the technical pro and cons, was that she hadn't taken the time to get to *know the customer* – to find out how Harry likes to buy. This was surely much more important to the outcome of the sale than Sally assuming Harry would want to know all the technical details – clearly she assumed too much! Consequently much of what Sally had to say had no effect in moving the sales process forward. Instead it lingered in a no-man's until Harry, seizing his opportunity, promptly left the building.

Now it goes without saying of course that meeting Harry's requirements would suit Harry, but it is certainly would not suit some other car buyers. Doubtless some would want to hear all the technical information. And this is probably the same person who is now defending Sally arguing that "knowing all the facts about each car would better enable Harry to make his decision." My response is merely to say; would it?

Well Sally certainly thinks so, but she was wrong in this case, though she would have been correct if it had been another type of customer. You see, not all customers are the same; they have different priorities. Harry's priorities were not based on technical specification, but model, colour and affordability. Sally failed to grasp this import fact so emphasised the priorities she deemed important.

What this example illustrates is that there exists a difference between *how* people sell, and *how* customers like to buy. More significantly it illustrates that *how customers like to buy is more important than how we like to sell*. This is an important point so I shall repeat it.

- *How customers like to buy is more important than how we like to sell.*

You see, and as I hope the example above has shown, how one person likes to sell is *not* necessarily how other people like to buy. Sally's *selling style* was technically based which was in opposition to Harry's pragmatic *buying style* – how Harry likes to buy. If Sally wants to sell more cars then she needs to be less concerned with her *selling style* and more concerned with her customer's *buying style*. These are two important terms to which I shall return later. First I want to address any remaining sceptics.

For anyone not yet convinced of the need to be aware of the customer's *buying style* let me try a little role reversal of the earlier example:

Suppose Harry is now the car salesperson and into the showroom walks Sally. Her passion for cars and how they work as it was before. Harry approaches and guides Sally to a selection of possible cars just as she had done for Harry previously. Sally then asks Harry the first of the many technical questions she requires answered, "How does the new hypertronic CVT compare with the CVT M6?" Harry's response is to say, "We only have the CVT M6 in stock." Now let's be honest, this might be true but it is not the answer Sally wanted to hear. What she wanted to know was the respective performance of the different models, not whether they had one in stock. So, like Harry before, there is a good chance that she too will leave without buying. And so she does.

The reason should by now be obvious. Harry, like Sally before, failed to grasp what the customer saw as their needs or priorities. In other words, he failed to get to *know the customer* - to understand how his customer likes to buy. For sure, price and availability are important to Sally, but so too was her desire or need to understand the technicalities of her possible purchase.

If we would be shocked by a doctor's frequent inability to make a proper diagnosis, when all the signs were there for the trained eye to see, then should we not also be shocked by a salesperson failing to make a proper assessment of their customer's *buying style*? For the trained salesperson all the signs are there to do so, as I will show, yet repeatedly they fail to spot them. Of course, the consequences of this failure might not be life or death, but there are consequences for such poor practice - poor sales performance!

So, Harry's failure was rooted in the same error as Sally's. And it amounts to this: they both attempted to sell in their *preferred selling style*, which happens to be the same as their *preferred buying style*. Yet in neither Sally's, nor Harry's case did their *selling style* match the *buying style* of the customer. If it had then we might have had a different outcome.

It might be objected that a salesperson never knows what type of customer they are dealing with, so how can they possibly know what the customer's *buying style* is likely to be. Well actually they can know, and I will be explaining later how this can be done. It is enough to say for now that the aim of this book is to show how it is possible to quickly identify how a given customer likes to buy – to identify their *buying style*.

But as I have already said, this is only half the job because how the customer likes to buy is not, necessarily, how we like to sell. For this reason this book will show the flip side of the coin as it were - how to modify our *selling style* so that buying style and selling style match. To put it another way; the aim of this book is to show how it is possible to sell to customer in the way they like to buy. Understanding this will go some considerable way to improving your personal closing ratio. Any improvement in our closing ratio is of course to the plus side of your ledger. On the other hand, to do nothing will be to the plus side of your competitor's ledger.

In case there remain any lingering sceptics about the need to modify their selling style let me just make this final point: among professional groups style modification is a way of life. Why it should be a subject barely, if ever, referred to in sales books is therefore surprising. Notwithstanding my continued amazement here are some examples of such professions:

The interior designer or architect will endeavour to say something about their client (be they individuals or corporations) in their designs and constructions. The Educationalist will ensure they teach in a variety of styles to appeal to the different ways in which people learn. The Lawyer will adapt their approach in the defence of a client to appeal to members of a jury, as will the Prosecutor. Marketing Executives the world over will spend weeks preparing just the right presentation to win over a particular client appealing directly to their likes, biases and so on.

In each case these professionals all instinctively, or through a conscious decision, attempt to anticipate what type of person or group they will be dealing with, and then adapt or modify their presentation accordingly. The better their perception of their target audience or market, the better the response they are likely to get, and therefore the greater the likelihood of a positive outcome. Now for any one of the professional groups mentioned, or any of the numerous other professionals who deal with people, to remain locked into a single approach toward all markets or audiences would be disastrous. So why should it be any less disastrous for us?

Before outlining how this book is structured I should add that the ideas outlined in this book have themselves evolved through discoveries made by both professional salespeople and trainers, and discoveries made by the behavioural sciences. Some of you may be familiar with models like learning styles by Honey & Mumford (1986) and Kolb (1976). Research that places an emphasis specifically on social styles has also been done. However, while this latter research focuses almost exclusively on observable behaviour. This book differs and instead focuses on mental states like desires and fears that actually cause behaviour. This is a subtle, but not insignificant distinction. It is the difference between polishing the outside of the car to make it perform better, or lifting the hood and adjusting the engine. There are literally dozens of other such models on the market and while acknowledging all the aim of this short book is quite simple: to help the professional salesperson improve their sales performance – nothing more. As a salesperson studying this guide you will be able to develop *selling styles* which not only focus upon the uniqueness of individual customers but, more importantly, identify their preferred *buying style*.

For the training professional this book will serve as means of teaching new salespeople the importance of understanding human behaviour, and thereby a means of managing the behaviour of others. This can only be achieved effectively by understanding how people behave, and thereby how they like to buy. In the absence of even a rudimentary understanding of human motivations the salesperson is left guessing, like Sally and Harry, with the attendant consequence of poor sales performance.

I begin in chapter one by stressing the importance and benefits of understanding personality styles for those involved in sales. This is followed in chapter two with a discussion on the need for versatility in dealing with customers of different behavioural, or personality styles than our own. Having provided in chapter three an overview of the four personality styles chapter four then provides a detailed account of the characteristics exhibited by each of these styles. This includes revealing their preferred environment, their characteristic mannerisms, vices, virtues and temptations. It will also be shown that there exists neither a single successful sales style, nor single sales type. Rather that there are only different types of people. Every personality type has its share of successes. Similarly, each personality type has both positive and negative characteristics, and each has different responses in favourable and antagonistic situations. It is the responsibility of each salesperson, perhaps with the aid of proficient trainers, to understand these differing personality types and use that understanding to help potential customers make a decision.

Using what you have learnt in the proceeding chapters in chapter five I will then show you how it is possible to identify a given customer's personality style. More importantly, how this personality style translates into a *buying style*.

So by the end of chapter five you will have completed the first of the two objects set at the beginning of this introduction. Namely, to explain why the gap exists between those sales you attempted to close, and those you actually did. However, achieving this first objective is, as I said, only half the task. In chapter six I provide a method by which you can identify your own selling style.

This groundwork is necessary before proceeding in chapters nine to twelve to show how each of the four *selling styles* needs to be modified to deal with the different customer *buying styles*. In studying the chapter relevant to your personality style you will have the tools to achieve the second objective – an improved closing rate.

Behavioural skills are not of course the only skills needed for success in sales. The successful salesperson will be the one who knows their business, knows how to plan and organise themselves, and finally, understands their behaviour and that of their customers. The first of these essential elements can be taught to the salesperson by a competent training organisation, or they can teach themselves. The second has been the subject of many excellent books accessible to anyone wishing to invest the time and money. The third is contained within these pages for those prepared take the time to understand how they sell and how customers like to buy.

Before I close this introduction let me just make a couple of brief points. Firstly, during the book I use the term 'customer' rather than 'client' 'prospect' or 'suspect'. This classification is intended to include all potential buyers of your product or service. This includes first time encounters with potential buyers, long-standing customers, and everyone in between. I also use the term 'product' throughout rather than 'service'. This is simply for ease and what applies to products applies equally to services.

Secondly, while this book is directed at salespeople and sales trainers its applications are far more reaching. Anyone in the business of persuasion, be it negotiating, marketing, training, or involved in the conversion to ideas, from the shop floor to the boardroom, will I believe find this book useful.

Enough said. Having outlined the intentions of the book and its scope it is now time to turn your attention to the business of understanding *how customers like to buy*.

Steve Deery    Nottingham 2013

# 1 - Understanding personality styles

## Why is understanding important?

Personality styles have held a fascination for thinkers of all kinds since antiquity. Our interest is concerns the importance of two elements required for success in selling as it relates to customers and their behaviour.

- The need to understand a customer's desires, fears, and motivations - without this understanding we can only guess as to why they do, or don't, buy from us.

- The need to recognise a customer's individuality - they are not all the same, so should not be treated the same.

While our objective in understanding personality styles is more mundane than that of our ancestors this does nothing to diminish its importance to the salesperson.

Human nature expresses itself in many forms of course and it is beyond the scope of this modest book to provide you with a complete understanding of human behaviour by way of personality styles. In fact complete understanding is beyond human capabilities. We cannot take a god's eye view of ourselves. The best we can do is to catch glimpses of ourselves - hints and clues as to who we are. But for all practical purposes this is all we need, with even modest advances in our understanding of personality styles enabling us to better function in the world. It opens up new possibilities for both personal and business growth.

Increased understanding of how we, and therefore how others, function leads us to toward greater *integration* as a person. This is the process where the customer's needs, fears, motivations and perceptions of reality count. Integration enables us to sell in a style that is in harmony with the *buying style* of our customers. The alternative to greater *integration* is of course its antithesis – the process of *disintegration*. This is the process where only our needs, fears, motivations and perceptions of reality count. Adopting this approach will though lead inevitably to failure - where self-interest prevails over co-operation. And no successful relationship can exist between a seller and a buyer in the absence of co-operation.

While it is often said we are all self-made it remains the case that we succeed in life to the degree to which we gain the support and co-operation of others. The converse is also true. We are unsuccessful to the degree to which we fail to gain the co-operation of others. Try selling to a customer without their co-operation!

If we are to pursue the process of integration then there are two aspects to understanding. The need to understand both the customer and ourselves.

What we gain from this joint understanding can be summarised as:

- It helps us as salespeople to identify our customers' *buying style.*

- It helps us as salespeople to identify our *selling style.*

Given that customer *buying styles* and our *selling styles* are explained in terms of *personality styles* we need first to understand the latter to understand the former.

## What is a personality style?

A *personality style* can be defined in the following way:

- It is a particular, persistent, manner in which a person expresses him/herself, either verbally or non-verbally.

Now, when we express this personality style as a customer's *buying style* we mean:

- The behaviour a customer persistently exhibits in all his/her verbal and non-verbal behaviour when buying.

And when we express this personality style as a salesperson's *selling style* we mean:

- The behaviour a salesperson persistently exhibits in all his/her verbal and non-verbal behaviour in the sales process.

So, understanding *personality styles* is the key to understanding *selling* and *buying styles.*

## Benefits of understanding

The benefits of understanding personality styles are then twofold. First, it enables us to identify a customer's buying style. In so doing we become more capable of reaching and understanding our customers. The second benefit is in enabling us to identify our *selling style.* This enables us to modify that *selling style* to match the customer's *buying style.*

Understanding also prevents potentially, or probable, self-defeating behaviour. All behaviour has consequences and as we gain greater insight into human behaviour through *personality styles* we learn to bring about positive, rather than random, consequences. These insights are crucial to achieving success in sales because they give us control over outcomes. Put simply, if we know that doing X produces Y results, and don't want the result Y, then we need simply stop doing X. It's not rocket science is it?

It is important to point out here that while understanding personality styles offers great benefits, temptation in the possibility of misuse is ever present. One such misuse would be a cynical attempt to manipulate a customer's emotions to gain a sale. Another might be the pretence to be something we are not in an attempt to try and win favour with the customer. Such ruses and deceits are not legitimate uses of our increased understanding. Indeed, they are prone to be regarded by the customer for what they are. Customers generally know when they have been manipulated and seldom are deceitful individuals capable of covering-up their true colours for long.

## A cautionary note

Having looked at the importance of understanding personality styles and its benefits it is now time turn my attention to the importance of the *versatility* understanding personality styles provides. But before I do I feel a few cautionary words are in order.

In attempting to produce a typology of personality styles the inevitably risk of over generalising is present. However, such generalisations are necessary. Any attempt to give a definitive account of *every* characteristic of human nature would require as many books as there are people! For this reason this book is *deficient* in its generalisations, but *sufficient* in its guiding principles. Let me explain. While on the one hand we are all unique we must also recognise that people often share certain basic character traits. A moment of reflection reveals both the similarities and differences we have with others. For example we are similar in those aspects which influence our character. These are such things as our language, culture, history and so on. Yet at the same time we are different as none of us is influenced in identical ways in our formative years. None of us are subjected to the same peer pressures, exposed to the same delights or traumas, and so on. Think also, for example, how pessimists all share the same basic character traits, as do all those we call optimists, depressives, and so on. Therefore, all of us can be recognised as unique, yet sharing similar chief or dominant characteristic.

With this thought in mind, I acknowledge the differences that exist between us, our uniqueness, but concentrate my attention in this book on the similarities, the character traits, or personality styles that make us in many ways similar. So let's begin considering the importance of versatility before beginning to unravel the differing personality styles in chapter three.

# 2 - The importance of versatility

In my introduction it was stated how unreasonable it would be for a salesperson to expect a customer to abandon their buying style in favour of their selling style. This would be like Harry, in our second example, expecting Sally to give up her expectation that the technical requirements for her new purchase be met. Ridiculous as such an expectation sounds it is often just the kind of expectation many salespeople have toward their customers. What is really required is *versatility* on the part of the salesperson. By versatility I mean simply the capacity to modifying our selling style to match the customers' buying style. This is simply a capacity to adapt in various situations. This capacity also exhibits a willingness to consider other ways of tackling a problem. As such versatility provides us with a many-sided approach to selling.

Consider for a moment the following sales situations:

- Should the technical-minded customer be satisfied with a salesperson's broad-brush explanations, or buyer benefits, about the product?

- Should the decisive customer be tolerant of the precise and systematic salesperson whose attention to detail would try the patience of Job?

- Should the flamboyant and forceful salesperson intimidate the conservative and cautious customer?

- Should the easy-going and affable salesperson irritate the restless and impatient customer?

None of these are reasonable expectations and in any one of these situations, or their reverse, the salesperson's natural selling style is alien, even hostile, toward the customer's natural buying style. Inasmuch as they are alien toward the customer they are detrimental to producing a successful outcome - a sale. If, instead, the salesperson practised versatility in their approach then each of these problematic encounters could be avoided.

In failing to adapt our selling style, to show versatility, to meet the customer's *buying style* we are like the obtuse Englishman abroad. The one who insists on speaking English despite the fact the Frenchman doesn't understand the language. The one who then blames the Frenchman when he fails to make himself understood! In such situations most reasonable-minded people would not expect the Frenchman to learn English. Similarly, why should we expect a customer to buy from us in the way we like to sell, rather than in the way they like to buy? It's absurd!

We might suppose such problems simply do not arise between speakers of the same language. How wrong we would be to make this assumption. Communication failure between salespeople and customers is much more common that we might imagine. How do we know this? Well, take your average salesperson. Now during the course of any given week they will present their product or service to any number of potential customers. Now, for various reasons not everyone buys. Perhaps it will be the wrong product, or the wrong price. Yet for some customers neither the product, nor the price will be an issue. So why will they not buy? Plain and simple, they will not be convinced. In other words, the salesperson will have failed to communicate how or why the product will benefit them, they may of course think that they did, but, self-evidently they hadn't, for if they had the customer would have bought.

Another way of checking this is to examine your own closing ratio. How many customers who could have bought, (i.e. price and product were not an issue), actually did? There will always be a gap and the bigger the gap, the worse the communication problem.

Given how widespread the problem is wouldn't it be better if we spoke the same language' - the one in which they are likely to buy. I call this language their natural buying style.

The responsibility for matching selling styles to buying style clearly must lay with the seller, not the buyer. Had we had all chosen a different occupation then perhaps things might be different.

Take being a Negotiator. Here it is not unreasonable to expect both parties to shift their style, especially if both parties are agreed upon finding a solution. Even in negotiations where no obligation exists to find a solution, and agreeing to disagree is an option, this doesn't provide any comfort for the salesperson. Agreeing to disagree with a customer seldom results in a sale! No sales manager worthy of the title is ever likely to pat you on the back if you return to the office announcing '*The customer and I agreed to disagree!*'

So how is the salesperson to respond to this responsibility? As individual salespeople we represent just one of four possible personality styles (these four styles will be explained in the following chapter). On the plus side this means our selling style will match the buying style of about one in four of our customers. On the downside of course our selling style is alien to the other three buying styles. The outcome of encounters with these three buying styles is likely to yield less than satisfying results. In order that they are successful we need to exercise versatility in our approach. We could of course pass the blame for all these missed opportunities at the door of poor sales skills; maybe we failed to identify the need, or maybe the customer was broke, who knows? Yet how many times have we identified a clear need for the product or service we were offering. Knew the customer could afford it. Yet still fail to come away with the order. Given how often this happens we could do worse than heed George Bernard Shaw's advice:

- The reasonable man adapts himself to the world; the unreasonable one persists in trying to adapt the world to himself.

In other words, we could do worse than adapt our selling style to match the customer's buying style. Be versatile!

We might all agree that tenacity is a desirable quality in a salesperson but to carry on selling in a style that alienates the customer is just a waste of effort. Adapting our selling style to minimise or even eliminate this conflict is therefore essential to our success. This requires a high degree of versatility on our part.

Isn't it the case that we find some customers to be friendly, yet others we find others are remote, some to be cautious, while others are prepared to take a risk. From this it follows that there is no one single selling style to suit them all. Neither, therefore, can there be a single selling style that is more successful than another. As I said in my introduction, it's not our selling style that matters but our customer's buying style. In each of the cases just described the buying style is quite different for each and you will need to modify your selling style accordingly if you are to win the order.

The problem that arises if you do not can be illustrated by the following example:
I meet Jane who has a buying style that I will characterise as rationale and objective. She prefers gathering, analysing and verifying the data before making a decision. And I, as the salesperson, have, say, a selling style that I will characterise as 'social'. I am bright and breezy in my approach and prefer not to dwell on hard facts. Here's a typical interaction between us:

**Jane**: *"How did you arrive at these performance figures?"*

**Me**: *"These are conservative estimates and I'm sure our product will satisfy your needs."*

Now my response seems plausible, to me anyway. But is Jane satisfied? No! This is because I failed to provide the verification she felt she needed. Her *How* question demanded a specific answer. My response was to breeze over it with a *What* statement (stating *What* the product will do, rather than *How* it was able to do it). The highlighted *How* and *What* employed here are what I term our '*organising priorities*', the other two being *Why* and *Who*. These *organising priorities* form an integral part of how each person sees the world and shape our personality styles. I will say more on *organising priorities* in chapter eight. For the moment it is enough to say that Jane and I clearly have a different way of seeing the world, she in terms of *How*, me in terms of *What*. Now unless I am able to satisfy what Jane sees as her priority, her need to know *How*, I am unlikely to get the sale. And there is little doubt that my answer was not the one she wanted. Quite simply I failed to exercise the versatility required to appeal to her buying instincts. So how might I have responded more effectively to Jane's question? How might I have demonstrated versatility? Let's try again:

**Jane**: *"How did you arrive at these performance figures?"*

**Me**: *"Let me show you the latest survey results published by an independent organisation. These show how the results were achieved."*

My response in this counterexample appealed directly to Jane's need to verify the facts given her. So regardless of my natural selling style I could have, if I had recognised Jane's buying style, tailored my responses accordingly to meet her buying style.

Having considered the practical aspects of versatility I now want to consider briefly the relationship that needs to exist between salesperson and customer. Selling is ultimately about establishing good relationships, not victory and defeat. To bring about positive outcomes - sales - and the effective salesperson should aim to secure two things. Firstly, the co-operation of the customer as we really can't do much without it! Secondly, ensure the well-being of a continued relationship with that customer. Without this second element we will fail to set-up tomorrow's sales. Viewing the sales process as a series of victories to be won, and defeats to be avoided, results in coercive actions being applied. Coercing, or pressurising, the customer to 'win' the order is hardly the basis for a long-term relationship.

So selling simply to secure our own substantive interests - the commission on the sale, or meeting the monthly quota - is a very short term and foolhardy strategy. The versatile salesperson strives for a synergistic outcome. This is an outcome where the combining of the separate elements of salesperson and customer unite to form something that would otherwise not exist - a regular and loyal customer on the one hand, and a committed and caring salesperson on the other.

Versatility therefore requires the salesperson to establish a dialogue with the customer, that is to say, an interaction in anticipation of ultimately agreeing on a solution. Having said this, given the different personality customers' have, attempting to establish a dialogue with them all has a downside. Most notably it means that we are without a specific 'sales pitch' - something we can learn by rote then deliver to everyone. Instead we need to become more fluid and adaptable in our approach, increasing or decreasing your levels of assertiveness, and or responsiveness, as each new encounter dictates.

However, this short-term downside is best endured as increased versatility leads to improved effectiveness. Here are just some of the problems high versatility can avoid:

- The low versatility salesperson remains domineering when to yield or seek approval would be more appropriate.

- The low versatility salesperson remains talkative when listening would be more appropriate.

- The low versatility salesperson is over familiar when being cool and detached would be more appropriate.

- Or, the reverse of any of these styles as each situation demands.

In short, selling in a single style, or low versatility, is limited. It reduces the number of customers we can effectively communicate with and therefore the number of sales we can make. The multi-styled, high versatility, salesperson in contrast extends their range of customers and improves the possibility of sales.

High versatility can be defined as:

- The ability to temporarily adjust our levels of assertiveness, and or responsiveness to encourage others to interact productively with us.

Whilst it is evident we are all versatile to some degree in our dealings with other people, and our level of versatility is reflective of how we currently communicate, there are also a number of other conclusions we can draw regarding versatility.

- Versatility is situational; no two situations are the same and we must adapt to each.

- The more versatile we are, the greater our ability to deal with differing personality styles.

The remaining chapters deal with these two aspects of versatility by demonstrating with situational examples how you can distinguish what selling style is appropriate in any given situation. I then go on to show you how to bring about mutually satisfying outcomes by appealing directly to differing customer buying styles. Before concluding this chapter there are two final points that need to be made.

The alternative course to modifying our selling style to match that of a customer's buying style is to sell within our own style. In other words, sell only to customers with the same orientation as us. Whilst this is not totally problem free as I will show (chapters 9-12) it would provide us with a market requiring less selling style modification. The downside though is that it will probably reduce our potential market by roughly 75%, even for those of who sell in niche markets. This is because no one market place has a monopoly on a given personality style and vice versa. In other words, all accountants are not the same, or chief executive officers, or marketing directors, or shopkeepers. In other words, no one occupational group attracts a single personality style.

Given that every salesperson seeks to gain the optimum results from every encounter it would seem logical to make some attempt to modify our selling style to ensure that we stand a reasonable chance of doing so. Admittedly this requires extra effort on our part, but then again, you cannot expect above average performance by being average!

The second and final point is one made in my introduction and I will repeat it here to reinforce my point. Among professional groups style modification is a way of life. For example, the interior designer or architect will endeavour to say something about their client (be they individuals or corporations) in their designs and constructions. The Lawyer will adapt their approach in the defence of a client to appeal to a particular jury, as will the Prosecutor. Marketing Executives the world over will spend weeks preparing just the right presentation to win over a particular client appealing directly to their likes, biases and so on.

In each case these professionals all instinctively, or through a conscious decision, attempt to anticipate what type of person or group they will be dealing with, and then adapt or modify their presentation accordingly. The better their perception of their target audience or market, the better the response they are likely to get, and therefore the greater the likelihood of a positive outcome. Now for any one of the professional groups mentioned, or any of the numerous other professionals who deal with people, to remain locked into a single approach toward all markets or audiences would be disastrous. So why should it be any less disastrous for us?

Having stressed the importance and necessity of a versatile approach to selling let us now begin the process of unravelling the differing personality styles.

# 3 - The four personality styles – an overview

Let me begin by re-stating the cautionary note given toward the end of chapter one. In attempting to produce a typology of personality styles the inevitable risk of over generalising is present. However, such generalisations are necessary. To attempt giving a definitive account of *every* characteristic of human nature would require as many books as there are people! For this reason you might say this book is *deficient* in its generalisations, but *sufficient* in its guiding principles. The caution hopefully noted it's now time to get to grips with the four personality styles.

The names assigned to each of the personality styles emphasis that particular style's most dominant characteristic. Being the most dominant characteristic it represents an individual's most significant strength but also, potentially, that person's most significant weakness. Whether or not this characteristic shows itself as a weakness or not will depend upon context.

For example, let us take the characteristic *patience*. Person *A* regards patience as one of their main positive attributes. This characteristic has served them well in their business, social and family life. However, during a crisis when quick decision-making was called for their extended deliberations became a liability rather than remaining an asset.

For others of course *impatience* is often regarded as a characteristic strength. Person *B* regards impatience (or 'quick decision-making' as they would characterise it to themselves) as one of their main positive attributes. Again they feel this characteristic has served them well throughout life in a variety of areas. Yet a little reflection may reveal that what you regarded as your main character strengths may also have been occasions when it failed you. Indeed, doing the opposite would have served you better.

The significance of these opening comments is twofold. First, it reinforces the idea that what we regard as character strength may not be seen as such by our customer. Second, it reiterates the obvious point that we do not all see the world in the same way, nor interact with it in a uniform manner. What some see as obvious other see as obscure, what some see as important others see as trivial, what some see as dull others see as exciting, and so on.

Clearly then we are not all the same, but then again neither are we all so different. It is in those areas where we share common traits that we get a toehold to understanding personality styles. For this reason the descriptions given for each style are approached thematically - that is to say they each relate to a theme, or shared characteristics.

This grouping together under a theme enables us to employ the short cuts used in trait psychology (e.g. to describe certain groups of people as 'disciplined', 'inquisitive', 'selfish', etc.) to handle the mass of information, including anxieties, interests, habits, and so on which go to shape an individual's character. Recurrent character traits are simply drawn together to reflect certain behavioural tendencies. The result is the assignment of personality style names reflecting shared behavioural patterns. These names are *Analytical*, *Drive*, *Amiable*, and *Expressive*, and are illustrated in diagram 1.

Each basic personality style has a natural *selling* style and natural *buying style* characterised by its dominant characteristics. As a salesperson, acting pre-reflectively, we would sell in one of the four styles that most closely resemble our dominant characteristics. In other words, we sell in either an Analytical style, or a Driver style, or an Amiable style, or an Expressive style. Now, should a customer share your personality style then, 'hey presto', our selling style will match their buying style. That's the good news. The flip side of the coin is that the remaining three personality styles, about 75% of the population, have a buying style that is alien, possibly even hostile, in relation to our selling style. This fact alone should reinforce the importance of versatility discussed in chapter two - our need to know how to modify our selling style in such situations.

You will also note from diagram 1 that those personalities to the right of the vertical axis are *Tell-type* personalities, whilst those to the left are *Ask-type* personalities. Furthermore, those above the horizontal axis are *Control-type* personalities and those below are *Emotive-type* personalities. These character traits are typical for each group and are expressed in this manner so you can easily identify the customer's basic personality style and your own. These important terms will reoccur throughout the course of this book and where necessary I will refer you back to diagram 1. However, it should be understood that each style's placement on the grid is important in stressing its relation to the other styles. The full significance of these relations should be apparent in chapter nine, hopefully before then.

So far then you know what the four styles are and that their positioning on the grid is significant. Now it is time to add some colour to this rough sketch. In chapter four I explain in detail the character traits attributable to each style. Given the emphasis of this book on customers in chapter five I will show how, using these four styles, you are able to identify a given customer's personality style. Knowing their personality style will give you an insight into their buying style. As you will recall from chapter one, understanding personality styles is the key to understanding buying and selling styles. These two chapters are only half the story of course, but more on that later. Now it's time to add some detail to the story so far. With this in mind chapter six will show you how to identify your personality style and the selling style it gives rise to.

## The Personality Grid

Diagram 1.

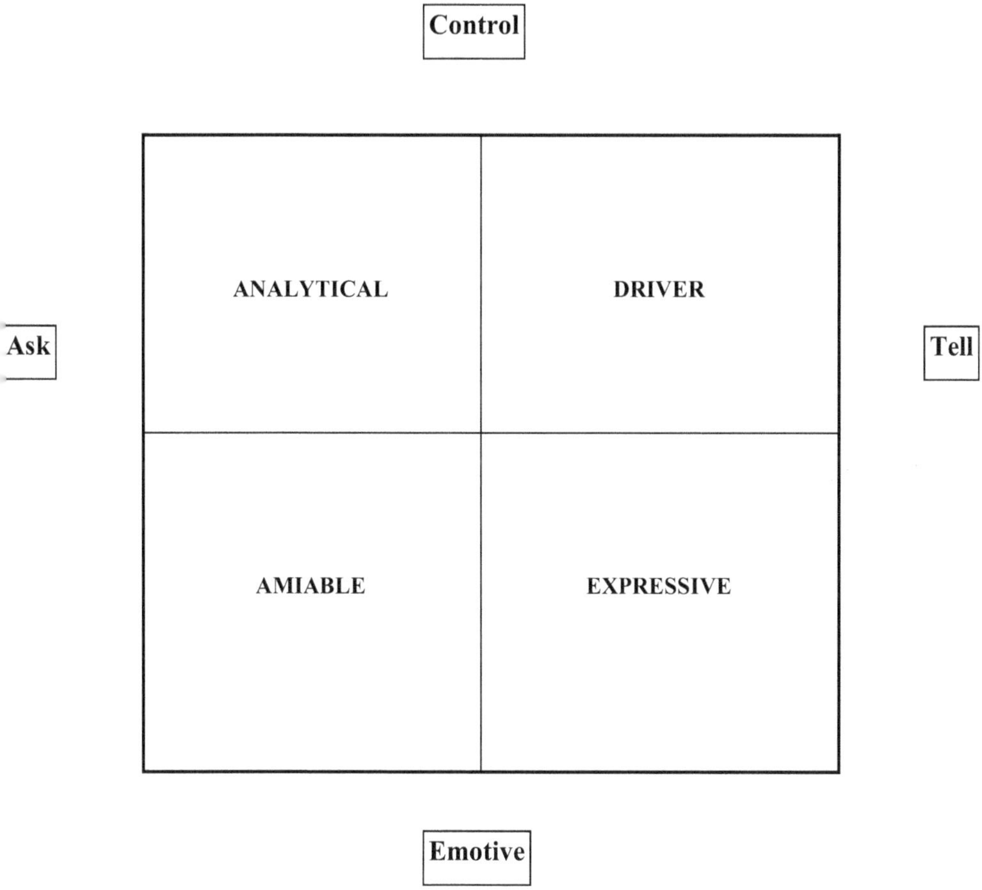

**Control**

| ANALYTICAL | DRIVER |
|---|---|
| AMIABLE | EXPRESSIVE |

Ask → / Tell →

**Emotive**

# 4 - The four personality styles – in detail

In reading through these four personality styles I would ask that you initially reserve judgement as to what you think is your particular style. Toward the end of this chapter a self-assessment tool will be applied to enable you to accurately plot yourself on the grid. Once done re-read the section relating to your plotted style.

## The Analytical personality

*Main characteristics*

The Analytical personality is characterised by a precise and systematic approach to tasks focusing upon key details. They have a tendency toward set procedures both in their personal and business affairs, and prefer working under known circumstances. As individuals they are tactful and diplomatic and will not intentionally alienate others. One might go so far as to say they avoid situations where conflict is likely.

Often described as the 'technical' personality, or 'Mr Numbers', they like to ask lots of 'hard fact' questions. In other words, they prefer questions about facts rather than feelings (see diagram 1). As critical thinkers it is their nature to be analytical and conservative and they spend time checking for accuracy. They are compliant toward authority. Their basic desire is to understand the world around them and their basic fear is to be overwhelmed by others (see diagram 9, and chapter 8 *Basic Desires and Fears*).

*Preferred environment*

This personality prefers things to proceed in an orderly manner and therefore likes a disciplined environment. They also like clear operational guidelines preferring to work as part of a department or group. Security and reassurance are both highly valued by the Analytical. In the work environment they prefer the status quo, unless reassured that standards will not fall by changing. It follows therefore that they dislike change and avoid risks. Those who notice and call attention to their accomplishments (especially their analytic ones) are also valued as their self-consciousness often prevents them from opening doors of opportunity themselves. As cool, or unemotional, personalities they are often indifferent to the agreement of others taking reassurance in the fact that having critically analysed the situation or problem they are right.

*Characteristic mannerisms*

This personality is recognisable by their slow deliberate manner. They are controlled both in respect of bodily movements and speech and may show signs of nervousness in both. They are not renowned for their quick action.

*Characteristic vices*

They are avaricious for knowledge and like to believe they have everything figured out and can therefore predicate probable outcomes. Confident in their reasoning ability makes it difficult, if not impossible, to persuade them that things might be other than they have concluded. The consequence of such stubbornness is that they can lose the very objectivity that characterises their personality.

*Characteristic virtues*
As discussed previously, a vice may also be a virtue and the Analytical is no exception. Consequently their enquiring mind enables them to see both sides of an argument before drawing their conclusions. Their problem-resolving skills enable them to rise above situations viewing them dispassionately and objectively rather than emotionally and subjectively.

*Characteristic temptation*
While objectivity has its place this personality tends to analysis everything and will often abstract themselves from the real world of emotions and feelings. In extreme circumstances they may become embroiled in the minute details which have nothing to do with the broader issues at hand.

*Summation*
The Analytical personality is a *high Ask* and *high Control* personality. This simply means they usually ask people to do things rather than tell them. It also means they prefer to be in control, so you will not find them readily expressing their emotions (diagram 1).

*Characteristics by which to identify the Analytical*

- Disciplined
- Compliant
- Careful
- Systematic
- Accurate
- Logical
- Reserved
- Suspicious
- Self-conscious
- Serious
- Avoiding (see diagram 2 for further character traits)

# The Driver personality

*Main characteristics*
This is a restless personality constantly in search of new challenges and immediate results. They are often unconventional and creative in their approach to problem solving. They are also renowned for setting high standards for both themselves and others and are often highly critical of those they feel do not attain them. Routine tasks quickly bore and irritate this personality and they abandon them in search of something more creative or spontaneous where quick decision making is called for. Decisions are not however based upon emotional impulses. Instead they prefer to gather the

facts, assess the risks, and then decide. They will often offer resistance to being part of a team, preferring instead to find self-tailored solutions to problems or challenges they encounter. In this way they can instigate actions rather than respond to events. Preferring to control rather than be controlled this type of person will resist supervision but compensates for this by being able to work effectively without close supervision - they assume authority. Ever questioning the status quo they are nonetheless prepared to take the responsibility for managing any problems that may ensue from the disruption.

Being both dominant and aggressive they are often described as a 'control' personality, or 'Mr Tough'. They ask bottom-line questions expressing little interest in formalities, or the 'why and wherefore', they also expect direct answers. This personality likes to get to the point quickly. For the driver self-reliance is paramount so it naturally follows that submission to the will of another is most feared (diagram 9, and chapter 8 *Basic Desires and Fears*).

*Preferred environment*
Being direct and forceful the Driver personality prefers a competitive environment constantly working toward the attainment of individualistic goals. They also dislike the limits imposed by rigid structures much preferring a wide scope of operations freed from controls and supervision. Environments which offer opportunities for the attainment of power and authority are preferred but so also is the opportunity for prestigious challenges where the possibility of failure or great success lay rather than certainty.

*Characteristic mannerisms*
The Driver personality is again one who has controlled body movements, and controlled and measured speech. Yet unlike the Analytical they exude an air of authority. They also expect others to accept their arguments. However, their impatience leads them to speak quickly about their ideas leaving behind those unable to keep up.

*Characteristic vices*
They possess an almost insatiable appetite for power. However, their striving for power can never be fully satisfied because limits are always imposed. The more they strive for power the more inevitably they will push boundaries resulting in rebukes. This is likely to bring about their basic fear of being controlled.

*Characteristic virtues*
As an outgrowth of their desire for control comes magnanimity - a selfless quality whereby they exercise control over their own desires to protection those they value. Their desire for self-sufficiency also acts as a check against possible megalomania inasmuch as they will realise that to totally control everything is just not possible, so they reassert themselves in a more balanced manner.

*Characteristic temptation*

Sometimes the Driver personality believes they are entirely self-sufficient. In its unhealthy extreme their self-interest prevails to the extent that they want to become so self-sufficient everyone will become dependent upon them. This is only tempered by their *characteristic virtue*.

*Summation*

This personality is *high Tell* and *low Emotive*. This person seldom *asks* and exhibits little *emotion*. So unlike the Analytical the Driver has no difficulty telling someone what to do. But like the Analytical they like to be in control (diagram 1).

*Characteristics by which to identify the Driver*

- Driving
- Competitive
- Forceful
- Inquisitive
- Self-starter
- Assertive
- Restless
- Impulsive
- Impatient
- Demonstrative
- Autocratic (see diagram 2 for further character traits)

## The Amiable personality

*Main characteristics*

The Amiable is by definition an easy-going and affable personality. Being content with things as they are they can often see themselves doing the same things years ahead. This makes them reliable, loyal and indeed predictable personalities performing consistently if not startlingly. They also prefer to be given directions rather than work on their own initiative. For this reason they prefer staying in one place performing tasks that require patience, concentration and skill. In their dealings with others they are indirect rather than direct. They are unpretentious and undemanding both in their working environment and socially and so able to get along with most people they encounter. They even have a calming influence on those around them who are more excitable. In respect to decision making they are prone to act upon emotion or popular opinion rather than fact and exhibit an aversion to high-risk situations. Friendship is highly valued and their family ties are very strong.

By virtue of their general demeanour and relationship-orientation, which makes them supportive, understanding and approachable, they are often described as the 'relator' personality, or 'Mr Warm'. Despite their intense like of others they are prone to be slow in coming forward socially. They are indecisive preferring to sit back rather than be a determiner of outcomes. They are also emotional people who will openly display their pleasure or displeasure. Again, the significance of relationships to Amiables tends to express itself in conversation – they will readily talk about people and their feelings. Their basic desire is to be needed or valued and to feel unneeded or undervalued is their most feared outcome (diagram 9, and chapter 8 *Basic Desires and Fears*).

*Preferred environment*

In respect to their working environment the Amiable prefers to plan their work carefully and then work at a steady well-ordered pace. They also like to get into a steady routine and do not respond to either disruptions or changes well. Equally, they dislike infringements upon their domestic life and for this reason have often been described as 'home bodies'. Territorially, then, they prefer to be based near to home. They also share a number of characteristics in common with their counterparts the Analytical (diagram 1) in that they prefer the status quo and value security highly. Because they value human contact highly sincere appreciation for a job well done, by a boss, partner or indeed anyone, is sure to be greatly appreciated. Whilst they remain appreciated they will always remain co-operative.

*Characteristic mannerisms*

Unassuming in nature the Amiable will tend to sit back, particularly in the presence of more assertive personalities, often adopting an acquiescent or subservient role. They are indecisive in nature and always concerned by who may be 'put-out' or upset by their actions.

*Characteristic vices*

Great satisfaction is derived from being self-sacrificing and virtuous. They believe in natural justice and that someday they will be rewarded for their humbleness and generosity. An extreme Amiable lives a life of martyrdom sacrificing their own desires and aspirations for others. This leads to them becoming inflated with their own self-importance believing that no one could cope without them. The problem arising from such extreme behaviour is that eventually they bring upon them their basic fear of being unloved.

*Characteristic virtues*

Amiable personalities have an unbounded capacity for disinterested charity - for helping others without expectation of reward or recognition. They exhibit great empathy with their fellow beings and can be relied upon in times of crisis to lend a helping hand, or a shoulder upon which to cry. Such genuine empathy and concern for others seldom allows them to deteriorate to the kinds of behaviour described above. As a consequence they can usually satisfy their basic desire to be valued and loved.

*Characteristic temptation*

The strong bias towards relationship-orientation leads this personality to believe they are always well intentioned toward others. This often leads them to deny they are in fact satisfying their own emotional needs and that it is necessary for them to behave in this manner. In so doing they are sometimes less well intentioned than at might first appear.

*Summation*
Once again we have a *low Tell* personality, like the Analytical, but one who is highly *Emotive*; yet different in that they readily express emotions. They are also in direct contrast to the Driver personality (diagram 1).

*Characteristics by which to identify the Amiable*

- Dependable
- Deliberate
- Amiable
- Easy-going
- Good listener
- Hesitant
- Undemanding
- Peaceful
- Conservative
- Overcautious
- Acquiescing (see diagram 2 for further character traits)

## The Expressive personality

*Main characteristics*
This gregarious and stimulating personality makes friends easily and demonstrates great social adeptness. They express themselves fluently and emotionally and enjoy entertaining people. Relationships are considered more important than results and so do not respond well to tight deadlines. Because of this emphasis on others this personality type often has difficulty in planning their time, they get distracted by their interest in others and are often reluctant to cut short friendly discussions for fear of offending the other party. Public recognition is also highly valued for this equates to social acceptance - the expressive likes to make a good impression. Competitive situations are preferred in providing yet another forum for recognition. Their decision-making ability is often based on intuition or impulse and this tends to lead them into quick decisions involving risk. Always willing to help others the Expressive can show great enthusiasm for others' ideas, as well as their own. Such unbounded faith may lead them to overestimate both their own ability and that of others. Preferring to be engaged in activities that require contact with others, or working as part of a team, they have an extensive network of contacts or friends.

This warm, approachable and likeable personality is often described as the 'socialiser' personality, or 'Mr Dealer'. They are easily recognised by their flexible, compromising and outgoing manner. Where there is an Expressive to be found there are sure to be others close by. Acceptance, then, is their deepest desire, consequently they fear rejection most of all (diagram 9, and chapter 8 *Basic Desires and Fears*).

*Preferred environment*

Because this personality places great importance upon relationships they are attracted to a working environment that gives expression to this desire - work and play must involve others. For this personality a people less and windowless environment is a hell. Being creatures of impulse they are at their best when freed from the constraints of control and detail. As a natural socialiser they enjoy opportunities to be in contact with others. This may be on a one-to-one basis, as they are naturals at coaching and counselling, or with a group. The group environment also affords the expressive the opportunity to receive any recognition that may be due publicly. With a dislike of hostile environments the Expressive is diplomatic in their approach to problems or challenges. To this end they would rather discuss proposals than implement them. Their natural enthusiasm also makes them good motivators. Populated environments are much preferred over those involving inanimate objects.

*Characteristic mannerisms*

This person is expressive in all respects often getting animated to emphasis a point. They are excitable people who speak quickly and with confidence willing and urging others to accept their ideas or opinions. Their conversation will, like the Amiable's, invariably relate to people and feelings.

*Characteristic vices*

The Expressive's popularity may lead them to believe they require no self-development. This is a delusion for what the public sees may only be a front or mask presenting the public with an image that is acceptable. The need for social acceptance may make them promise more than they can deliver. Consequently their inability to say 'No' causes them to over-stretch themselves; saying 'No' might bring upon them their worst fear of being rejected. Whilst being extremely friendly individuals friendships are often not very deep. What they may really want is your acceptance, not your friendship.

*Characteristic virtues*

The healthy Expressive exhibits high self-regard based upon their abilities and qualities. Their genuine like of people makes it almost impossible for them to exploit others or exhibit hostility. Such leanings naturally lead the Expressive to express a genuine love of people for which they are genuinely liked and accepted.

*Characteristic temptation*

The Expressive personality may feel the need to present a 'larger than life' image to maintain their high self-esteem and feelings of superiority. Yet often a gap may exist between the real person and the outward persona.

*Summation*

In the Expressive we have a *high Tell* personality, like the Driver, yet unlike the Driver they are *highly Emotive* personalities. This is in direct contrast to the Analytical personality (diagram 1).

*Characteristics by which to identify the Expressive*

- Charismatic
- Influential
- Affable
- Verbal
- Persuasive
- Impetuous
- Active
- Energetic
- Restless
- Impulsive
- Attacking  (see diagram 2 for further character traits)

These descriptions of the personality styles show clearly that not everyone is the same. But neither is everyone so different. Given both difference and similarity it should come as no surprise that the buying styles of these styles differ from each other. But simply knowing this is of little use unless we are able to match a given customer to a given style. To this end we must now turn.

# Shorthand description of the basic styles

Diagram 2.

| ANALYTICAL PERSONALITY | DRIVER PERSONALITY |
|---|---|
| Slow reaction<br>Minimum concern for relationships<br>Cautious action<br>'Get it right' attitude | Swift reaction<br>Minimum concern for relationships<br>Direct action<br>'Get it done' attitude |
| Exacting<br>Serious<br>Critical<br>Indecisive<br>Deliberate<br>Logical<br>Disciplined<br>Cautious<br>Emotionless<br>Precise | Thorough<br>Severe<br>Dominating<br>Decisive<br>Requiring<br>Efficient<br>Controlling<br>Intolerant<br>Competitive<br>Authoritative |
| Respectful<br>Supportive<br>Dependable<br>Awkward<br>Unassuming<br>Emotional<br>Cautious<br>Indecisive<br>Careful<br>Willing | Personable<br>Enthusiastic<br>Gregarious<br>Undisciplined<br>Manipulative<br>Emotional<br>Impulsive<br>Competitive<br>Spontaneous<br>Demonstrative |
| AMIABLE PERSONALITY | EXPRESSIVE PERSONALITY |
| Unhurried reaction<br>Minimum concern for change<br>Supportive action<br>'Let's do it together' attitude | Rapid reaction<br>Minimum concern for routine<br>Impulsive reaction<br>'Let's get it done' attitude |

# 5 - Identifying customer styles

No single personality style has a monopoly over a particular profession. This having been said, certain career paths do attract predominantly one type - Analyticals to the Sciences - Expressives to the Arts, and so on. But to assume that *all* scientists are Analyticals or that *all* marketing executives are Expressives is a misconception. So, while a person's occupation may give clues to their underlying personality style, and therefore their buying style, this information alone is insufficient to draw any firm conclusions. There are also many occupational groups that give us no real clues to a person's personality style. Given these problems it is imperative we gather additional evidence. This evidence comes from two sources, a person's verbal behaviour and non-verbal behaviour.

Before profiling the behavioural patterns of each personality style there are some other influences that need to be understood:

- Customers do not function in a vacuum so consequently their behaviour may be influenced by numerous factors.

- The customer may have been instructed by a superior to gather specific information about our product which they themselves may not necessarily be interested in. Consequently their questioning may not be reflective of their personality but their superior's.

- The customer may only be a 'spokesperson' and not entirely convinced that what they have been instructed to buy is right. As a result they may lack any real conviction which will influence both their verbal and non-verbal behaviour during the sales interview.

- If the sales meeting is held in the presence of colleagues the customer may attempt to portray the image expected of them, rather than their real personality. Therefore, they may act tough or authoritative because they feel this is how they should behave, rather than because they feel naturally inclined to do so.

- Not least of all, our own verbal and non-verbal behaviour may influence them. How we dress, how we look, how we speak, and how we behave all produce a reaction in others.

On this last point; any one of the above factors may trigger an underlying prejudice the customer has which causes them to respond in a biased, discriminatory, jaundiced, chauvinistic, sexist, or even racist manner. Alternatively we may evoke a reaction which is peculiarly favourable because of our physical attractiveness, accent, race, sex, and so on which may evoke similarly anomalous behaviour in the customer. Whilst we cannot greatly influence the immediate reaction we evoke from others we can exert some degree of control over our reactions which may be just as anomalous. We are not immune from behaving in a prejudicial or favourable manner toward customers either because of their immediate qualities/defects. However, by reacting in a habitual or unreflective manner we introduce distortions into the meeting just as the customer might - pre-judgements which imposes limits upon the sales presentation and thus its scope. To avoid these prejudicial/favourable responses we need to become non-judgmental responding to what we actually experience, rather than what we believe to be true or immediately perceivable.

Bearing in mind these various considerations we must both observe the customer's physical behaviour, and listen intently to what they say and how they say it, in order to elicit those vital clues that 'unmask' the 'real' customer. Is the customer active? Do they gesticulate as they speak? Are they controlled and restricted in their movements? Do they speak quickly or slowly? Are they open and friendly? Are they reserved and cautious? What sort of questions do they ask? Are they fact-orientated questions? Are they bottom-line questions? Personal questions? Identifying these vital clues early on in the sales presentation enables us to determine what the basic desires and natural buying style of our customer are and so respond accordingly.

To assist you in identifying what type of customer you are dealing with each style is profiled in turn. These brief profiles are in part a summation of those already outlined in some depth in chapter four. Included within these brief profiles is a section entitled 'Typical occupations'. Having already said that all types of personalities are to be found in all types of occupations, and therefore a customer's occupation should not form the sole basis of a character assessment, certain occupations do attract certain personality types. Therefore, occupation may be your first, and I emphasis first clue, to a customer's personality style. Also included under each personality type are sections entitled 'Characteristic behaviour', and 'Typical questions asked'. By attending to these few pointers it is possible very early on in the sales process, possibly even at the point of first contact on the telephone, to establish a customer's personality style.

The three remaining sections under each profile are incorporated for general guidance purposes when dealing with this personality style. However, you should study the relevant style modification chapter (either 9 10, 11, or 12 as it relates to you) where these sections are duplicated. Reading the relevant chapter as suggested provides a more comprehensive guide to dealing with different personality styles in a sales situation. At the end of this chapter I provide a quick summary for each personality's buying style. This is, however, only a guide and should not be read instead of the following profiles.

## Identifying Analytical customers

*Typical occupations*
The type of occupation preferred by a customer with an Analytical personality is one that involves details and planning. Occupations dealing with 'things' rather than directly with people. Typical occupations would be actuaries, accountants, computer technicians and programmers, engineers, scientists, chemists, researchers and technicians.

*Characteristic behaviour*

The Analytical is often recognisable by their slow deliberate manner. They are controlled both in speech and in bodily movements often exhibiting nervousness in both.

*Typical questions asked*
- *How* long has your company been established?
- What qualifications do you have?
- *How* many clients do you have?
- Do you have audited accounts for your company I can examine?
- What guarantees can you give me?
- Can you substantiate those claims?
- What evidence do you have?
- Can you explain *how* that works?
- I do not have to decide now, do I?
- Is this a proven product?

*Response guide*
Analytical customers are cautious and often suspicious individuals. 'Yes' or 'No' answers in response to questions are seldom sufficient. Therefore, you must answer all questions fully, providing documentary evidence whenever possible to support your claims. Speak slowly and in a controlled manner to match the vocal inflexion of the Analytical.

*Questions to ask*
- What are your thoughts on this so far?
- Do you see *how* this will work?
- Would you agree that the evidence is conclusive?
- Can you think of any points we have not covered?
- What conclusions would you draw from this?

*Areas to avoid*
A firm handshake is fine, a slap on the back is not. Avoid getting too familiar or too personal in your questioning. Glib or shallow answers to questions raised are fatal if you are seeking to build trust and confidence. Avoid last-minute surprises as they are not well received.

## Identifying Driver customers

*Typical occupations*
A customer with a Driver personality would most likely choose an occupation where tangible results can be obtained. Environments that offer either the opportunity for power and authority, or actual power and authority, are ones in which Drivers are likely to be found. Typical occupations would be executive officers, salespersons and sales managers, business managers and owners and politicians.

*Characteristic behaviour*

Controlled in both speech and bodily movements, like the Analytical, but exuding in confidence and authority. Impatience on the part of the Driver leads them to be brusque in their dealings with others.

*Typical questions asked*
- *What* is it you want to show me?
- *What* does it do?
- *What* will it cost me?
- How much time will this take?
- *What* would happen if...?
- How soon can you put this into effect?
- *What* guarantees can you give me?
- Is this the best on the market?
- Is it new to the market?
- When can I get it?

*Response guide*

The Driver wants you to get to the point quickly and does not want long-winded answers to their questions, 'Yes' and 'No' answers are often sufficient. They want you to be business-like, efficient and brief. Stick to the main product features or bottom-line results. Speak with confidence and authority.

*Questions to ask*
- How do you feel you can best achieve your objectives?
- *What* have you done about them so far?
- Which option do you believe best achieves your objective?
- Is this agreed?
- When do you want it by?

*Areas to avoid*

Do not be indecisive when dealing with this type of person, they want you to provide them with answers, not problems. Inefficiency is not looked upon favourably so do what you say you will, or do not offer at all. Do not bore them with detail, take care of them yourself whenever possible.

# Identifying Amiable customers

*Typical occupations*

The Amiable customer prefers working within a highly structured and predictable environment with as few variations in their routine as possible. Typical occupations would be administrators, civil and social services, production, teaching and computing.

*Characteristic behaviour*

The Amiable personality is an unassuming and quiet character who will often take the subservient role in the presence of a more forceful character. They are indecisive although not nervy. Their bodily movements whilst not controlled are not animated like the Expressive.

*Typical questions asked*
- *Why* should I buy from you?
- Have many other people have bought this product?
- This is a safe product isn't it?
- How long has your company been in business?
- How long have you been doing this job?
- Can you assure me of this return?
- How often do you make service calls?
- There is no rush to decide, is there?
- Can I discuss this proposal with my friend/spouse?
- Can I think it over for a week or so and get back to you?

*Response guide*

The Amiable personality likes things to be taken slowly and wants to be sure you are trustworthy. Answer their questions fully, while at the same time demonstrating that you genuinely care about them. Provide proof of your answers whenever possible. Speak in a slow non-threatening manner.

*Questions to ask*
- *Why* do you feel that way?
- *Why* is that important to you?
- Do you feel this is the right thing to do?
- Do you feel we can work together on this?
- Can you see *why* this is the right course of action?

*Areas to avoid*

Avoid rushing or cajoling the Amiable. Show patience and tolerance and in this way earn their trust and confidence. Be firm and friendly, but not insensitive to their feelings

# Identifying Expressive customers

*Typical occupations*

The Expressive personality likes to work in situations that require motivating and influencing others. They also prefer to work freed from controls and rigid routines. They also like to compete and are often found in occupations which allow them to give expression to their individuality. Typical occupations would be in coaching, sales, counselling, marketing, advertising, acting and the Arts.

*Characteristic behaviour*

The Expressive personality is often recognisable by their animated bodily movements, including facial expressions. They are excitable people who speak quickly, enthusiastically and confidently.

*Typical questions asked*
- Can we meet and discuss this over lunch?
- Do you mind if I bring along a friend to sit in?
- Is this a new product?
- I like the sound of that, but could you explain that part again?
- It sounds a bit complicated?
- Can you do it cheaper?
- Shall we finish our discussion over dinner?
- I want to show it to a friend before I decide. You don't mind do you?
- I like the sound of that, would you do all the paper work for me?
- Will it be you I deal with in the future?

*Response guide*

The Expressive personality would much prefer to socialise than talk business. Their questions often reflect a personal desire to be friendly - so reciprocate. Keep factual answers regarding the product simple, if you can get away with a 'Yes' or 'No' answer then do so. They are not overly concerned with proof, or facts and figures so keep them to a bare minimum covering only the main product features. Speak with enthusiasm and become animated too.

*Questions to ask*
- Am I right in assuming you will make the final decision?
- Your colleagues will feel the same way I'm sure, don't you agree?
- Based upon your knowledge of the subject which solution do you feel works best?
- I feel I can work with you on this, how do you feel about me?
- Shall I take care of all the necessary paperwork for you?

*Areas to avoid*

Do not allow this type of customer to distract you from the true purpose of your meeting by talking too much. Do not bore them with procedure - just take care of it.

## Identifying customer buying styles

In chapter one it was said that understanding personality styles enables us to determine a customers' buying style. This is because the customers' buying style is explainable in terms of their personality style. In chapter four the four styles were presented in detail and so far in chapter five we have applied this understanding to help identify a given customer's personality style. It only remains therefore to explain the buying style derived from these personality styles.

## Analytical buying style

- They dislike small talk and prefer to get down to business quickly.

- They like to take time when buying in order to absorb and weigh-up all the facts.

- They need to be shown evidence in the form of hard facts to support any claims made about your product.

- Testimonials are useful to the Analytical provided they are from another Analytical source.

- They are cautious when it comes to the new or innovative.

## Driver Buying Style

- They hate to waste time preferring instead to get straight down to business, in a business-like manner.

- They like hard facts but prefer to talk about the main features of a product rather than the minute details.

- They like to know what the benefits of a product are - what it will do for them or their business.

- They dislike problems and prefer to hear what solutions you have.

- They like to buy new and innovative products and are prepared to take risks for high rewards.

## Amiable buying style

- They prefer to take things slowly and buy from those whose trust has been earned.

- They like to see the facts and figures related to your product and to understand each in turn before moving to the next.

- They like to talk about their personal interests and to get to know you before buying.

- They will want assurances that you are trustworthy and may require additional visits to secure that trust.

- They prefer to buy products with a proven track record and low risk threshold.

## Expressive buying style

- They prefer to focus on the main features of a product and have little time for minor details.

- They prefer exciting and imaginative sales presentations to the slow and methodical.

- They like to do business in a friendly way and often in a convivial environment.

- This personality prefers the new or innovative product and is willing to take risks.

- For this personality social proof that your product works is often better than statistical proof.

## Concluding comments

In chapter one I said there were two advantages to understanding personality styles:

- It helps us as salespeople to identify our customers' buying style.

- It helps us as salespeople to identify our selling style.

With chapters four and five complete the first of these potential advantages should now be an actual advantage. But as my closing comments to chapter three suggested, this is only half the story. To make use of this new knowledge we need to realise the second of those two advantages. But before we can complete this second phase of understanding we first need to identify your personality style. By the end of chapter six you will know what your particular selling style is, and so have the key to your selling style. Chapter seven merely adds refinement to your understanding. In the remaining chapters you will be shown how to apply this new knowledge in the field.

# 6 - Identifying your basic style

Having read chapter four you may by now have a pretty good idea of what your personality style is, as these styles apply equally to you. Alternatively you may well feel that at any one time you are any number of the personalities described. By the end of this chapter you will be in a position to settle the matter.

The self-assessment tool used at the end of this chapter to confirm individual personality styles is very simply. This is not intended as an apology as it is sufficient for the purposes of positioning you on the personality grid (diagram 1). However, for those whose curiosity has been aroused numerous personality-profiling systems are available on the market. But as I stated previously, my intention has not been to provide a definitive personality testing or measurement system. Rather my purpose has been to provide you with a simple, but effective, tool to aid effective communications between you and your customers.

Before asking you to complete the simply self-assessment test I would ask that you heed a few cautionary words as it is possible to misidentify yourself. Correct identification is essential if your particular selling style is to be matched successfully to a customer's buying style. Failure to correctly plot your style will simply not do when in chapters nine to twelve you begin to apply what has been learnt.

Misidentification can occur for a number of reasons. Firstly, people often choose the personality style of the type of person they would like to be, rather than the one they are. A person with low self-esteem may choose the personality style they feel gives them power and prestige in the eyes of their peer group. The lonely person may choose the style that seemingly endows them with likeable qualities. Such mistakes are common so you need to be objective in your self-assessment if you are to gain any insights and subsequent benefits. Whilst complete objectivity is not possible it is a time for being honest.

Another common error is to use the various lists of character traits as a sort of pick 'n' mix; selecting those traits you deem most complementary or desirable. However, personality styles are not arbitrarily constructed; from each style evolves other traits expressing the desires, fears and values of that personality. This is why you often find contradictory traits for a given style. These contradictory traits provide a counterbalance to prevent each style from becoming maladapted but instead to remain within certain characteristic limitations.

It is also worth reminding you of my introductory comments about not falling into the trap of thinking there are 'success types'. So do not fall into the trap of picking the personality style you think is most likely to succeed in sales. No one grouping has a monopoly on success in sales, indeed the world's top salespeople are to be found within each of the groupings.

Having noted these cautions, and studied the various traits, hopefully one style will present itself to you as the one most reflective of your basic style. There may well of course be traits that you do not readily recognise. This doesn't mean that they are not reflective of your personality. We are all disposed to reject those character traits we deem undesirable, and embrace those we think desirable. A close partner will often confirm what we ourselves are naturally inclined to deny – ask them.

Not all errors in assessment are so easily avoided of course. Given that different personality styles have character traits in common mistakes are easily made. So important is the issue of misidentification it is worth taking the time to identify the more common errors in detail.

## Misidentifications

The first two potential misidentifications are between those personality styles that are diametrically opposed, or 'opposites'. These are the Amiable and Drive, and Expressive and Analytical.

### *Confusing Amiable with Driver and vice versa*

Having read the profiles for the respective styles it seems difficult to comprehend that anyone might confuse the easy-going Amiable with the hard-nosed Driver, but such misidentifications can and do occur. Being forceful and domineering; two traits which distinguish the Driver most readily, are not character traits monopolised by Driver personalities. The Amiable can also exhibit similar traits under certain conditions. Where an Amiable holds a position of responsibility which necessitates they exhibit leadership they too can become forceful and domineering. Although the Amiable never attempts to dominate in a direct and open manner, as the Driver does, they do try to dominate under the guise of concern for others. Where they differ of course is in intent. It is for power for the Driver and emotional control for the Amiable.

### *Confusing Expressive with Analytical and vice versa*

These two personality types are another pair of 'opposites' who exhibit a similar character trait that might lead to misidentification.

In order to extend their sphere of influence, or to be seen as originators of new concepts, the Expressive may attempt to pass-off borrowed opinions as their own well considered judgements. In other words, they may give the impression of being 'thinkers', which of course is a major distinguishing characteristic of the Analytical. This is not to deny that the Expressive is original or an intelligent individual, on the contrary, they are often very creative. However, exhibiting one major trait similar to the Analytical does not make them an Analytical. The style of thinking differs markedly.

Analytical personalities are detail-orientated people who are curious for curiosity's sake. They may spend months, even years, getting to the core of a problem without thought of recognition or reward. The Expressive on the other hand originates ideas for recognition, fame and riches and wants to be recognised for their achievements.

Expressives also lose interest very quickly, moving on to some new theme once they have exhausted its possibilities, or see more scope for recognition in some other idea. In 'thinking' the Expressive pursues knowledge with another goal in mind, whereas thinking for the Analytical is the pursuit of knowledge for its own sake.

This, it must be admitted, is very much a one-sided misidentification. No one would ever confuse an Analytical for an Expressive yet the possibility of misidentification the other way around can occur, so beware.

The next set of misidentifications are perhaps more easily understandable as they fall either side of the vertical axis which distinguishes Ask-type personalities from Tell-types (diagram 1).

By virtue of being more closely related than those personalities diametrically opposed they share more common characteristics and are therefore more easily confused with each other.

*Confusing Expressive with Driver and vice versa*
Both Driver and Expressive are competitive and ambitious personalities. However, their primary motivations differ. For the Driver it is self-sufficiency and power, for the Expressive it is recognition (see diagram 8). These differing forces lead each to pursue their ends in different ways. For the Driver this will be without regard for the sensibilities of others, whereas the Expressive will be ever conscious of others for fear of bringing upon themselves their basic fear of being rejected. They also compete at a fundamental level for different things. For the Driver it is intangibles such as power and authority, for the Expressive it is for the tangible trappings of success which they believe will boost their esteem in the eyes of others.

Despite both personalities being characterised by their competitive nature there is a striking dissimilarity is their respective attitudes toward rejection and failure. The Driver is not concerned about what other people think of them, so long as they get what they want. They also see failure as an integral part of succeeding, or as part of the learning process if you like. In contrast, the Expressive cares greatly what other people think so will consciously avoid situations that could lead to rejection. They will also avoid the possibility of failure fearing this will result in a loss of popularity or social acceptance.

This common misidentification is again largely one-sided. The Driver knows exactly what they will, and will not, do. Therefore this is a misidentification often made by the 'aggressive' Expressive who sees themselves as a power broker believing this adds glamour to their image. In reality though the Expressive shares less with the Driver than might at first seem apparent. For this reason the 'aggressive' Expressive personality needs to examine more closely their underlying motivations and not the gloss that seemingly adds lustre.

*Confusing Amiable with Analytical and vice versa*
These two personalities share more than a tendency to 'Ask' which causes misidentification to occur (see diagram 1). You will recall from the descriptions given previously that the Amiable can be inclined to overrate their own importance. Analytical personalities also share the same basic tendency. The Amiable regards themselves as a stalwart of emotions. For the Amiable this means trying to carry everyone's emotional baggage. They may even believe that without *them* holding things together no one could cope. However, Analyticals overrate themselves for a different reason. They believe no one else understands problems as well as they do. So despite this mutual tendency to self-importance the distinction between them becomes apparent when you examine the basic motivation behind their behaviour. For the Amiable, emotion rules, for the Analytical, intellect rules.

Both personalities also share a similar attitude toward change much preferring the status quo to constant change. But again their motivations differ. For the Amiable they see change as a potential infringement upon their personal life. For the Analytical change is purely a distraction from existing clearly defined operational guidelines.

Both personalities are also indirect in their dealings with others. For the Amiable of course this lack of self-assertion emanates from a desire to be liked, but for the Analytical it emanates from the certainty of their reasoning. This means for the Analytical there exists no basic desire to be accepted - it is enough for them to know the 'truth'.

The shared low risk threshold might also cause possible misidentification. Therefore it is important for you to investigate further your primary motivation. This is to be loved or valued if you are an Amiable, and to understand how the world works if you are an Analytical. Ask yourself the following question: *Am I more concerned with feeling or emotion?*

The next pair of potential misidentifications can be found either side of the horizontal axis distinguishing 'control' from 'emotive' personalities (diagram 1). First, those who are 'control' orientated.

*Confusing Analytical with Driver and vice versa*
Both character styles exhibit individualism by setting themselves apart from everyone else. But the motivation behind this act is completely different for each. The 'aggressive' Analytical will set themselves apart because of their superior understanding or knowledge. You will recall that the Analytical seeks control through knowledge. Self-sufficiency in the form of control is not however a defining characteristic of the 'normal' Analytical, but it is one common to all Driver personalities. Therefore to take the desire to control as the sole trait by which to identify your style can easily lead to misidentification occurring.

Both personality types share similar basic fears, but they are not the same. Being overwhelmed by others in the case of the Analytical is not the same as Driver's submitting to the will of others (see diagram 8). This might be better appreciated by referring back to the basic desires outlined for each. For the Analytical it is to understand the world around them rather than be overwhelmed by it. Whereas the Driver aspires to self-sufficiency believing any threat to this requires them to give up some control over their destiny. Possession, then, is an outgrowth of control for each but once again of differing things - knowledge or self.

Despite apparent similarities the Driver is unlikely to be confused. The misidentification is more probable from an 'aggressive' Analytical who has introduced distortions into their reasoning.

However, an area where both styles might make misidentification is in respect of their attitude toward others. Both are emotionally detached and therefore independent. Neither requires social acceptance to confirm their existence, nor indeed to justify their actions. Both will act upon their respective objectives (I hesitate to use the word 'goal' as the Analytical is not goal orientated in the same way Drivers are) regardless of the opinion of others. But again the difference is marked. The Analytical simply does not need other people and may even reject social involvement. The Driver on the other hand does need people, despite often denying it, to achieve their objectives is apt to totally ignore the feelings of others.

Now to our finally pairing who are both to be found on the 'emotive' side of the horizontal axis (see diagram 1).

*Confusing Amiable with Expressive and vice versa*
Once again we have apparent similarities in behaviour but as outlined in the previous section their underlying motivations are the real key to distinguishing one from the other. If the two previous personality styles above can be distinguished by their self-interest, then the Amiable and Expressive can be distinguished by their concern for others. This does not mean that these two personalities are distinguishable by their concern toward others' welfare. It is rather the case that they can be more concerned with how others feel about *them*. For both, what other people think and feel about them is important and the motivations behind this are the means by which you distinguish one from the other. For the Amiable their motivation is to be loved or valued. However, the Expressive is less concerned with your devotion but rather with your perceiving them favourably.

As a result of their respective motivations both personalities are prone to bouts of self-deception. The Amiable believes they are primarily concerned about others, but is really concerned with satisfying their own emotional needs, or, even worse, adding fuel to their belief they are indispensable. Expressives who delude themselves do so by creating a larger than life figure that even they eventually cannot live up to.

Feelings of jealousy or envy can also be experienced by both personalities. The Amiable can be jealous of those they have 'invested' emotion in. The Expressive can be envious of others success. Both personalities can of course exhibit genuine feelings toward their fellow beings. The well-balanced personality is committed to others and this offers them the opportunity to reveal more of their true personality and thereby gain greater self-esteem.

## Personality Style Grid

Having read through the guidance notes on misidentification you may still be wondering how such distinct personality styles could get confused. This is primarily because not all personalities fall neatly into each category but can be positioned on the personality grid close to another style. Here their style is less distinctive, even taking on the behaviour of their *sub-style*. I will say more about *sub-styles* in chapter seven but for now you should understand the personality styles well enough to be able to plot yourself on the personality grid.

Before doing so let me repeat briefly my initial cautions: Do not pick the style you want to be. Be as dispassionate and objective as you can. Having plotted yourself on the personality grid do not reject it when re-reading the basic style profiles in chapter four simply because you dislike some of the less complimentary descriptions. Remember, self-knowledge, requires recognition of your potential vices as well as your virtues. If you feel uncomfortable about certain 'vices' then this may be an indicator as to your style. This is because the truth or potential truth about ourselves often hurts which is why we expend a great deal of effort in life hiding our real motives from everyone, including ourselves.

## Completing the personality style grid

- Read the guidance notes for diagram 3.
- Then circle one of the four letters on diagram 3 below to indicate your assessment.
- Read the guidance notes for diagram 4.
- Then circle one of the four numbers on diagram 4 below to indicate your assessment.
- Remember there are no right or wrong answers, only honest ones.

## Guidance Notes – diagram 3

This assessment measures your level of assertiveness.

*Assertiveness*
Definition: The amount of effort you make to influence the thoughts and actions of others. Are you demanding, aggressive, assuming, confident, or domineering? Or are you reflecting, timid, apprehensive, irresolute, or modest?

'D' reflects low assertiveness, an Ask-type personality. 'A' reflects high assertiveness, a Tell-type personality (diagram 1).

In making your decisions compare yourself with the population as a whole rather than against a single person. Otherwise this may produce an over or under-estimates of your levels of assertiveness. This is most likely to occur when an individual is closely associated with someone at either end of the continuum, a boss or spouse perhaps.

**Level of assertiveness**

Diagram 3.

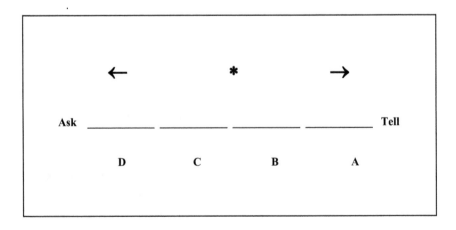

# Guidance Notes – diagram 4

This assessment measures your level of responsiveness.

*Responsiveness*
Definition: The amount of effort you make to control your emotions when dealing with others. Are you cool, dispassionate, reserved, undemonstrative, or indifferent? Or are you warm, passionate, tempestuous, demonstrative, or attentive?

'1' reflects low responsiveness, a 'Control' personality. '4' reflects high responsiveness, an 'Emotive' personality (diagram 1).

In making your decision once again compare yourself with the population as a whole rather than against a single person as this may produce over or under-estimate of your responsiveness.

**Level of responsiveness**

Diagram 4.

Having made your two choices plot them on the grid (diagram 5) where the two points intersect.

The decision C 3 for example would be plotted as indicated by the *X* on diagram 5. This person would be described as a 'Driver/Amiable' (indicated in red). In other words the basic style is Amiable with a Driver sub-style. Again I will say more about sub-styles in chapter seven.

Please remember this tool is only intended to serve as a guide to assist you in the field of sales by providing insight into different personality styles. Armed with this insight you are able to appreciate the impact your personality style has on the different styles your customers will exhibit and modify it accordingly.

If you are still unsure of your style it might be worth taking a moment to simply reflect upon your basic desires and fears. Are you driven to be right - to understand the world about you? Are you driven by a desire for self-reliance? Are you driven by the desire to be loved? Are you driven by the desire to be accepted or admired?

In respect of those feelings which cause you anxiety or stress. Do you fear being overwhelmed? Do you become aggressive when you feel you are not in control? Are you fearful of being alone in the world? Does the prospect of failure make you feel unworthy as a person? Having considered, now plot you position.

## Plotting your personality style

Diagram 5.

| D | C | B | A |
|---|---|---|---|

| Analytical | Driver | Analytical | Driver |
|---|---|---|---|
| **ANALYTICAL** | | **DRIVER** | |
| Amiable | Expressive | Amiable | Expressive |

1

2

| Analytical | **Driver** *X* | Analytical | Driver |
|---|---|---|---|
| **AMIABLE** | | **EXPRESSIVE** | |
| Amiable | Expressive | Amiable | Expressive |

3

4

**I see myself as a/an** ..................-.....................
(Sub-style here) (Basic style here)

If you have made your assessment I recommend you now re-read the basic styles descriptions in chapter four to get a clearer indication of your personality style.

Having satisfied yourself that you have accurately identified your personality style and plotted this, along with your sub-style, we now need to identify your selling style in the same way customers buying styles were identified in chapter five.

## The four selling styles

In chapter one I said that understanding personality styles will enable you to determine your *selling style*. This is because selling styles are explainable in terms of personality styles. In chapter four the personality styles were presented in detail and so far in chapter six we have applied this understanding to help identify our personality style. It only remains therefore to explain the selling styles derived from these personality styles.

## Analytical selling style

- They dislike small talk and prefer to get down to business quickly.

- They like to take time when selling in order to present all the facts.

- They like to provide evidence in the form of hard facts to support any claims made about their product.

- They are cautious when it comes to the new or innovative.

## Driver selling style

- They hate to waste time preferring instead to get straight down to business, in a business-like manner.

- They like hard facts but prefer to talk about the main features of a product rather than the minute details.

- They like to talk about what the benefits of a product are – what it will do for the customer or their business.

- They like to sell new and innovative products and are prepared to offer high risk products for higher rewards.

## Amiable selling style

- They prefer to take things slowly.

- They like to show the facts and figures related to the product and to explain each in turn before moving to the next.

- Likes to talk about their personal interests and to get to know you before selling.

- They prefer to sell products with a proven track record and low risk threshold.

## Expressive selling style

- They prefer to focus on the main features of a product and have little time for minor details.

- They prefer exciting and imaginative sales presentations to the slow and methodical.

- They like to do business in a friendly way and often in a convivial environment.

- This personality prefers selling new or innovative products.

- This personality will tend to offer social proof testifying to the worth of the product rather than statistical proof.

You will be quick to note that these selling styles are almost identical to the buying styles outlined at the end of chapter five. The reason for this is simple - how you buy is how you would sell, or alternatively how you sell is how you would buy. This should come as no surprise given that both styles are derived from the underlying personality style, and this style remains constant regardless of whether you are buying or selling - only the context changes.

# - Basic styles & sub-styles

Understanding sub-styles not only provides greater understanding of how the basic styles function but, more importantly, it will enable more subtle interactions to take place between you and your customer. Your sub-style (unless you are plotted on an outer-quadrant) also provides the possibility of insight into the other styles motivations/desires/fears, etc. This can be invaluable if your customer's dominant style matches your sub-style.

Having completed the self-assessment in chapter six you will now have an *X* plotted in one of the sixteen quadrants shown on diagram 5. The four main quadrants represent your personality or *basic style*, with their four sub-divisions representing *sub-styles*. Understanding these *sub-styles* will prove invaluable for style modification discussed in chapters nine to twelve. From chapter four we know what the four basic styles are. But what does it mean to have a basic style with a sub-style?

If your *X* were placed as indicated by *A* in diagram 6 you would be described as a 'Driver-Driver' personality. If your *X* were placed as indicated by the *B* in diagram 6 you would be described as an 'Analytical-Driver' personality.

It should be noted that when describing a given style we refer to sub-style first then the basic style, with the sub-style acting as a modifier on the basic style. You will no doubt have already noted this when writing down your style in the space provided in chapter six.

Tell

**Personality Grid - Sub Styles**

Diagram 6.

|  | Analytical *B* | Driver *A* |
|---|---|---|
| **ANALYTICAL** | **DRIVER** | |
|  | Amiable | Expressive |
| ——AMIABLE—— | ——EXPRESSIVE—— | |

In the two examples given the basic style remains the same, so both personalities share the dominant Driver characteristics. Yet while both are Drivers their sub-styles differ. In the case of the 'Driver-Driver' they exhibit only Driver characteristics because their basic style *is not* modified by any sub-style (it too is Driver). On the other hand, the 'Analytical-Driver' possesses sub-Analytical characteristic in addition to their dominant basic-Driver characteristics, so their behaviour *is* modified by their sub-style. Putting it simply, not all Drivers are the same.

What applies to the 'Driver-Driver' also applies to the other personalities which are positioned in the outer quadrants of the personality grid. In none of these cases is the basic style modified by a different sub-style. However, positioned in any of the remaining twelve quadrants mean the basic style *is* modified by a different sub-style. For example, the 'Expressive-Analytical', 'Amiable-Driver', 'Driver-Amiable', 'Analytical-Expressive', and so on (C2, B2, C3, B3 respectively on diagram 5) are all basic styles modified by a sub-style.

So how does this affect our selling style? Those of us with personality styles positioned at the extreme corners of the personality grid will need to make the greatest modifications in our selling style to match the buying style of those customers positioned elsewhere on the grid. The reason for this is we have nothing in common with any of the other styles by virtue of our sub-style.

The position is only marginally better for personalities positioned elsewhere on the grid. While we will have something in common with some of our sub-style counterparts (our customers whose basic-style matches our sub-style) it still excludes all the other possible personality styles. So while we will have to make less modification in our selling style to match a customers buying style we will still need to make numerous modifications.

So, all personality styles will need to modify their selling style, it is only a matter of degree depending on where we are placed in relation to a given customer.

The reason why all the personality styles will need to make some style modifications when selling is because how we see ourselves is not how others perceive us. Take the 'Driver-Driver' for example. Typical adjectives used by a third party to describe this personality might be *aggressive, blunt,* or *harsh*. However, the adjectives we use to describe ourselves might be *determined, single-minded, efficient, or decisive*. In reality, both personalities are one and the same - it is just a matter of perception. In sales of course there will always be at least two perceptions. Below is a set of first and third party description for each of the four main personality styles is provided to emphasis the extent of the perception problem (diagram 7).

There exist, however, a special set of problems for those personality styles positioned in the outer quadrants. To illustrate the point let us take two 'extreme' personality styles: an 'Analytical-Analytical' representing the customer, and an 'Expressive-Expressive' representing the salesperson.

## See yourself as others see you

Diagram 7.

| ANALYTICAL | | DRIVER | |
|---|---|---|---|
| *Customer* | *You* | *Customer* | *You* |
| Critical | Industrious | Domineering | Determined |
| Indecisive | Serious | Pushy | Single-minded |
| Moralistic | Orderly | Harsh | Thorough |
| Stuffy | Vigilant | Severe | Decisive |
| Exacting | Persistent | Blunt | Efficient |
| AMIABLE | | EXPRESSIVE | |
| *Customer* | *You* | *Customer* | *You* |
| Comforting | Agreeable | Manipulative | Talkative |
| Retiring | Dependable | Undisciplined | Dynamic |
| Awkward | Supportive | Hysterical | Personable |
| Dependent | Willing | Reactive | Enthusiastic |
| Ingratiating | Concerned | Excitable | Stimulating |

These personalities are diametrically opposed and we can see this when comparing just a few of the adjectives used below to describe each, in fact they are almost the antithesis of each other.

**Expressive-Expressive**    **Analytical-Analytical**

- Undisciplined            Disciplined
- Persuasive               Unassuming
- Impulsive                Careful
- Trusting                 Suspicious
- Self-promoting           Self-effacing

Indeed, so un-alike are these two personality types that one wonders whether they can stand to be in each other's company at all. But as we know, you can't always choose your company. The problem here for the Expressive-Expressive salesperson is that the *buying style* of the Analytical-Analytical customer is just the complete opposite of his selling style. The customer makes decisions based upon facts that must be logically outlined and presented, and done so in an unemotional and rational manner. This is because reason and not emotion is dominant for this personality.

On the other hand the Expressive-Expressive would rather skip the detail and focus on the main product features. Moreover, he will try to establish a relationship with the customer based upon personality, feelings, rather than facts. Now unless our salesman modifies his approach the prospect of a successful outcome looks unlikely. More likely he will annoy the customer with 'irrelevancies'.

So, even from this simple illustration we see that to achieve the best possible outcome from each sales meeting it makes sense to know our customer. This means knowing their buying style, knowing our selling style, and knowing what is required of us to bridge the gap, and in some the gulf, that exists between the two. The first two of these objectives have been achieved in chapters five and six respectively. It now remains to consider the final and most significant element which makes practical use of what we have learnt – the process of modifying our selling style.

# 3 - Modifying your selling style

## What's involved?

For any given personality style there are two components, namely the 'core' and 'adaptive' elements. The 'core' is that part of a personality that has evolved over the years and is characterised by a person's characteristic temptations outlined in chapter three. This aspect of our personality changes, if it changes at all, slowly over a prolonged period. Should we ever attempt to force change upon ourselves for whatever reason, it is these characteristic temptations which resist us until we finally, if ever, overcome them.

The 'adaptive' component is that aspect of our personality over which we can exert some degree of control for short periods. This 'adaptive' element is what enables us to adapt your selling style to match a customer's buying style. The process involved is similar to that used to modify our 'normal' behaviour when, say, in distinguished company, attending a job interview, meeting prospective in-laws, and so on.

Exerting control over this 'adaptive' element in order to modify our selling style, requires knowing what we are *changing from* and what we are *changing to*. From the preceding chapter it should now be clear what we must *change from*. In this and later chapters we will be examining what we will need to *change to* if we are to successfully interact with the variety of different customer's buying styles. It perhaps does not need saying, but in deciding what to *change to* we should adopt only the positive characteristic of that personality style. In other words, the *characteristic virtues* of a particular style (Chapter 4). To become highly contentious when a customer disagrees with the 'facts', or become imposing, or become self-promoting, or become suspicious, are all *characteristic vices* to be avoided.

## What's at stake?

It needs no stating either, but is worth reminding ourselves, that the objective of all salespeople is to achieve an outcome that satisfies not only their *substantive* interests, but also secures an interest in the *relationship* with their customer. To pursue outcomes that secure only their *substantive* interests is in essence a win/lose approaches where they are willing to secure the deal at any cost. In the absence of these two guiding principles then intimidation and pressure become the guiding principles.

Attempting to secure only an interest in the *relationship* is a lose/win approach. Here the guiding principle becomes accepting only what the customer will offer - any deal will do. In this type of meeting pressure is exerted in the opposite direction with the salesperson trying only to preserve harmony between themselves and the customer.

Pursuing either of these two courses may result in a sale being made of course, but ultimately both are lose/lose outcomes. This is because neither approach lays the foundations for a synergistic process whereby both parties' needs are fully met. Another aspect of these two approaches is that they both invite a higher probability of a short-term lose/lose outcome where no sale at all is made. This is because both parties invite one side to make concessions the other may not ultimately be willing to make.

The professional salesperson in contrast is one who has concern in equal measure for both the *substantive* and the *relationship* aspect. Behaviour that is reflective of these joint concerns is characterised by a search for common interests - problem solving behaviour where the interests of both parties are met. Here both parties collaborate to find mutually satisfying solutions to their needs.

However, such relationships should not be regarded as compromise arrangements whereby one meets the other halfway, or trades concessions. These are similarly lose/lose situations as the object of both parties is merely to avoid conflict rather than be involved in a synergistic problem solving process.

A successful selling style is one that offers the greatest possibilities to both parties, one that results in the highest quality sales and the most satisfying relationships.

Some might argue it is always their intention to satisfy these twin outcomes. However, the behaviour of some toward the customer often suggests otherwise. Regrettably some salespeople engage in behaviour that reveals their true motivations - concern for their own substantive interests, or alternatively, concern with the preservation of the relationship regardless of their own substantive interests. If synergistic outcomes are not to remain in the realm of mere good intentions we must avoid discrepant behaviour that negates them. To do this we must develop new skills to bring it about and we can begin by modifying our selling style.

The discussion in chapter two was I hope persuasive but in the event it fell short in its objective let us remind ourselves why our basic selling style is alien toward certain customers' buying styles. The following examples should illustrate the potential mis-match between selling and buying styles.

## What's the problem?

*Driver toward Amiable customer*
The Driver has a tendency to get straight to the point and places little emphasis upon developing a relationship - they hate to 'waste time'. What the Amiable would prefer is to take time establishing a relationship before getting down to business. Basically they want to do what the Driver regards as irrelevant. The Driver is also highly interested in new or innovative products. The Amiable on the other hand is slow to change preferring to stick to what they know rather than change for what to them seems like change for change's sake.

*Amiable toward Driver customer*
The Amiable salesperson is inclined to spend time trying to get to know the Driver customer, making them a friend, before attempting to sell. This tries the patience of the Driver who just wants them to get to the point quickly and cut out what to them seems irrelevant.

*Analytical toward Expressive customer*

Being a rather cool and unemotional character the Analytical salesperson focuses on the facts during a sales presentation. They rely upon these rather than themselves to win the order. This approach is too remote for the Expressive who would much prefer to discuss the general, not the specific. In fact, the Expressive is more interested in *who* you know than *what* you know. In short, Analytical salespeople will bore the Expressive customer

*Expressive toward Analytical customer*

The Analytical is a naturally suspicious character feeling justified in their suspicions if the Expressive refuses to talk hard facts. The Expressive's reliance on their sheer force of character to win the order, rather than the facts, is likely to alienate the Analytical. They will seem frivolous. The Expressive's enthusiasm for the new or innovative product will also meet an unreceptive audience in the Analytical who prefers the tried and tested. Once again we have a case where the selling and buying styles don't match.

From these simple contrasts in personality styles it should now be evident our selling style will be alien toward the preferred buying style of some customers. As such what we deem important is not always what others deem important and this difference means we organise ourselves to respond to the world in different ways. These different ways I call our *organising priorities* (diagram 8).

## What do our customers see that we don't?

How we take account of a customer's *organising priorities* will be explained in the chapter relevant to your personality style. What is required here is to briefly explain what is meant by *organising priorities*.

Each personality style differs in their motivations and these differences are reflected in what each style perceives as being the most important consideration. Moreover, these motivations determine how we see the world and what we value as important. For example when the Analytical is considering the merits of buying say a car, they are concerned principally with the technical aspects - *How* the car works, or *How* the financing works. They are least concerned with *Who* else might own such a car. Here what they value is not expressed in terms of others but in terms of knowledge.

In complete contrast to this style is the Expressive who is principally concerned with *Who*. Here the emphasis is upon the personal - with status for example. They are least concerned with what goes on underneath the hood - the *How* of the car. So, unlike the Analytical, value is expressed in terms of others. In the case of the Driver *What* things do is more important than *Why*. Here what they value is expressed in terms of functionality. This contrasts with the Amiable whose interest or valuation is expressed in terms of *Why* and least in terms of function, or *What*.

The emphasis placed on a single organising priority does not mean the other priorities are irrelevant, on the contrary. In each case all four organising priorities are important. So for example the Expressive, though primarily motivated by the *Who*, may still be highly interested and knowledgeable about the technical aspects of cars. However, the *How* issue is of less importance to their decision-making process than *Who*. So, all four of these organising priorities are of importance. What differs is the order in which they are internalised for each personality style. In diagram 8 the order is given for each style.

If we share with a customer the same personality style then our organising priorities will also coincide. If however, we have a different set of organising priorities we will place a different emphasis on the *How, What, Why,* or *Who* depending on our personality style because we will view the world differently.

It should be clear that in placing the emphasis on the wrong organising priority for a given customer we fail to identify what is important to them, and sell based on what we consider as most important. And quite frankly, what we see as being the most important consideration counts for very little in the sales process!

In each of the four chapters that follow we will consider further what each style's organising priorities are, and what we must change them to, in order to appeal directly to a given style's motivations. Doing this ensures that every sales presentation we make is geared directly to the organising priorities of that customer. Failure to do this just will not do.

**Organising priorities**

Diagram 8.

| ANALYTICAL | DRIVER |
|---|---|
| How-What-Why-Who | What-How-Who-Why |
| **AMIABLE** | **EXPRESSIVE** |
| Why-Who-How-What | Who-Why-What-How |

# What do our customers desire and fear?

Having grouped individuals by the shared characteristics under our four style headings we can deduce from their values (i.e. their organising priorities) shared desires and fears. For example, the Expressive's organising priority makes pre-eminent *Who*. The emphasis, and therefore value, here is in terms of others, or relationships. As relationship orientated individuals it follows that the basic desire shared by all Expressive personalities is to be accepted. And if this is their shared basic desire then it follows they also share its antithesis, the same basic Fear of being rejected. Naturally any one individual will have other idiosyncratic desires and fears. For example, Amanda may desire to retire at fifty, and fear getting lung cancer. However, these are not character traits. So reference here to desires and fears applies only to those shared character traits.

Diagram 9 below shows the basic desires and fears for each personality type and should be borne in mind when considering how to appeal to our customers' different buying instincts, or buying styles, in the subsequent chapters. We can however summarise the importance of understanding these desires and fears by saying that as individuals we are motivated by our desires, and seek to avoid bringing upon ourselves our fears. Moreover, in appealing to our customers' desires rather than their fears they are more likely be receptive toward us. When selling to customers it is therefore imperative that we direct our efforts toward their desires and not their fears. Put this way of course it seems to make perfect sense. Yet, as I have tried to stress throughout this book, our selling style often appeals directly to customer fears rather than desires. This is particularly so in the case where our customer has a style diametrically opposed to ours, but it also applies to those of the same personality style. I will say more on this in the subsequent chapter. Now it is time to move on to more practical matters.

## Basic desires & fears

Diagram 9.

| ANALYTICAL | DRIVER |
|---|---|
| **Basic Desire**<br>To understand the world around them | **Basic Desire**<br>Self-reliance |
| **Basic Fear**<br>Being threatened or overwhelmed by others | **Basic Fear**<br>Submitting to the will of others |
| AMIABLE | EXPRESSIVE |
| **Basic Desire**<br>To be loved, needed or valued | **Basic Desire**<br>To be accepted |
| **Basic Fear**<br>Being unloved, unneeded or under-valued | **Basic Fear**<br>Being rejected |

## What to do next?

It is advisable to read only the suggested modifications in chapters 9-12 relating to your own personality and selling style. This will avoid confusion, apart from which no insight will be gained from learning what those with selling styles different from your own will need to do.

# 9 - Modifying your Analytical selling style

## Your selling style in brief

A facts and figures salesperson much prefers to sell established products with a proven track record. You are somewhat reserved and do not get emotionally involved with your customer. You are also an independent thinker who formulates their opinions having weighed-up both sides of the argument; consequently you enjoy acquiring new knowledge.

## Selling to Driver customers

In many respects you have characteristics similar to that of the Driver customer in that you are both cool characters who have no desire to make the sales process personal. Instead you prefer to remain business-like. Another positive aspect of your selling style is that being organised you are unlikely to bring to the sales process matters which detract from the issues at hand. You excellent organisational skills also mean you are not likely to leave loopholes in your presentation for the Driver to pounce on.

Another strong point in your favour is that you will not make promises or guarantees you cannot keep. Furthermore, you are unlikely to try and direct or bully the Driver customer. This would be a direct appeal to the Driver's basic fear of submitting to the will of others and therefore likely to be countered by them with equal force (see diagram 9).

Seemingly, then, there is a lot you do naturally when selling to Driver customers that should ensure a successful sales presentation. However, there are other aspects of your natural selling style likely to alienate Driver customers.

*The Sales Presentation*
Your preoccupation with facts makes you inclined not to think in terms of outcomes - *What* a product will do. Instead you tend to concentrate on *How* the product will achieve it. However, for Driver customers the *What* is more significant than the *How* and therefore you need to put more emphasis on the *What* during your sales presentation in order to appeal to their natural buying style (see diagram 8).

Having studied all the facts relating to your product you are prone to come to a meeting with ready-made solutions to the customer's problem. But it is important to note that Driver customers prefer to make their own decision. Remember, their basic desire is for self-reliance. To avoid legislating for them you should provide alternative solutions for them during the course of the presentation. This makes the Driver feel they have retained control and so appeals to their buying style.

During your sales presentation you can become too immersed in the detail of the product trying to ensure every 'i' is dotted and every 't' crossed. But while this might be important to you in your attempt to be thorough it does not appeal to the Driver. They will regard your 'thoroughness' as a distraction from the big picture. For the Driver customer the bottom-line is their major concern, all they need or want to know are the high points or main features of your product and can often base their decision to buy on these alone. Recall that self-reliance is pre-eminent for this type of customer. Where minor details need to be ratified the Driver may well delegate these to a subordinate to deal with. Details, therefore, whether they are presented in the form of statistics, projections or testimonials need to be highlighted only as they serve to focus on the bottom-line. To repeat - the Driver is more interested in *What* a product does rather than *How* it will achieve it - placing emphasis on the wrong issue will not appeal to the Driver customer's buying style.

Disagreements can arise over facts because of your certitude; you are then inclined to become contentious or abrasive with those you regard too 'stupid' to grasp the information. Given that if anyone is likely to challenge you it is a Driver customer you might be inclined to respond by attempting to win the 'intellectual argument' rather than the order. You may of course win the argument, but only by getting the Driver to submit to you which only appeals to their basic fear. This would of course be a rather futile exercise because your job is to win orders, not arguments. When challenged you need to exercise self-restraint remaining focused on winning the order, not the intellectual argument. This means avoiding the Driver's basic fear of submitting to your will.

Another area of possible contention between you and the Driver customer is your respective attitudes toward risk. You prefer to sell the tried and tested product that minimises risk, whereas the Driver's buying instincts are toward the new and innovative with their inherent risk. So when it comes to offering solutions to problems appeal to the Driver's buying style by ensuring the potential rewards are high enough for them, too small and they will not buy. It is important therefore that you relax your natural reserve and become more adventurous in your problem solving.

*Response guide to questions*
The Driver wants you to get to the point quickly and does not want long-winded answers to their questions, 'Yes' and 'No' answers are often sufficient. They want you to be business-like, efficient and brief. Stick to the main features of your product or bottom-line results. Speak with confidence and authority.

*Questions to ask*
- How do you feel you can best achieve your objectives?
- *What* have you done about them so far?
- Which option do you believe best achieves your objective?
- Is this agreed?
- When do you want it by?

*Areas to avoid*
Do not be indecisive when dealing with this type of person. They want you to provide them with answers, not problems. Inefficiency is not looked upon favourably so do what you say you will, or do not offer at all. Do not bore them with details take care of them yourself whenever possible.

*Closing the Sale*

If having succeeded in steering clear of most, if not all, of the major pit falls when presenting to the Driver customer do not revert to type at the point of closing the sale. Do not procrastinate believing the logic of your case is a self-evident truth which the customer is compelled to accept and act upon by asking for the order form – they won't. The last thing you want to avoid appearing to be when in front of a Driver is ambivalent about whether they should buy or not. You need to be decisive but at the same time allow the customer to feel they are making the final decision – this is how they like to buy! An alternative close delivered confidently is often sufficient; *"Tell me, which would you prefer...?"* and then go straight to completing the order form

*Organising priorities*
You are inclined to adopt a selling style based upon the following priorities: The *How-What-Why-Who*. To sell to the Driver customer you need to re-arrange your priorities in the following sequence: The *What-How-Who-Why*. Remember, drivers are concerned with *What* a product will do rather than *How* it will do it. Moreover, they must feel that in buying *they* will achieve the objectives or solution offered by your product.

**Snapshot Profile**
- You have a *How* selling style. The Driver customer has a *What* buying style (see diagram 8)
- The Driver's *Basic Desire* - Self-reliance
- The Driver's *Basic Fear* - Submitting to the will of others (diagram 9)

## Selling to Amiable customers

Those aspects of your respective characters that are similar once again allow for common ground between you to be attained naturally. Where your selling style and the customers buying style coincide are principally in the areas of low assertiveness, attitudes toward change, and low risk threshold. But you will recall from our discussion on misidentifications that the emotional basis for you as an Analytical and the Amiable differs and because of this your selling style needs to be modified. However, to continue for the moment with those shared similarities. You are not inclined to be too domineering or demanding and this will appeal to the Amiable customer, whose basic desire is feel needed (see diagram 9). Neither will you be inclined to offer innovative solutions to problems which again will appeal to their preference for the tried and tested. The assurances and guarantees you might offer when selling will always be substantiated and this will secure for you the Amiable customer's trust and confidence.

Despite these similarities it is, as already stated, your differing primary motivations which necessitates you modifying your selling style in order to appeal fully to the Amiable customer's buying style. They have a basic desire to be needed while your basic desire is to understand and emphasising your desire as opposed to theirs can be costly.

*The Sales Presentation*
Your inclination to get to the heart of the matter, the facts as you see it, needs to be tempered when selling to Amiable customers. The heart of the matter for the Amiable is truly their heart, not the

cold facts relating to your product. For this reason you should begin your sales presentation with a personal rather than factual comment and thereby appeal to their basic desire, not their fear.

Because of your self-assurance, based upon your product knowledge, your natural selling style is to assume everyone will see the logic of your presentation clearly and then proceed at pace. But this would be too quick for the Amiable. The Amiable customer likes to buy having taken time to digest the facts. This may lead to you becoming impatient with yet another 'stupid' customer. This impatience needs to be curbed and you should be prepared to take more time explaining the facts, and you must do so in an informal rather than authoritative and, to them, threatening manner. Remember it is to their basic desire you must appeal.

Should disagreements arise during the sales presentation resist the temptation to restate the facts of the case. The Amiable will probably not fight back whatever you do, but will feel unneeded or unwanted if you are seen to be dismissive. Whenever possible provide the Amiable with personal assurances and clear, specific, solutions that offer maximum guarantees.

Another area of your natural selling style requiring attention is your impersonal approach. The Amiable is an emotional person and needs to be shown you have a sincere interest in them as the prefer to buy from people they like. Showing you care, not faking it, can be achieved by finding areas of common interest, or by being more open and warm with them. Ask them about their family and hobbies, the things they regard as important, and do not rely solely upon your facts and figures to win them over. This would be to appeal to your basic desire.

Because the Amiable customer is similarly cautious they are inclined to ask questions before buying. You will respond positively to this but you should avoid responding as if dealing with another Analytical. Respond instead with questions that draw out the Amiable's opinions and attitudes. This will be greatly appreciated by the customer as it shows you genuinely care about them.

Avoid coming to the sales meeting with pre-packaged solutions. The solution you have worked out may be the right one, but rather than laying it out for the Amiable customer draw out their goals and listen to them. Having listened respond to their needs by working with them to show how your solution can help them achieve their objectives. This approach will be received and responded to warmly because it appeals to their desire to be needed.

*Response guide to questions*

The Amiable personality likes things to be taken slowly and wants to be sure that you are trustworthy. Answer their questions fully, while at the same time demonstrating that you genuinely care about them. Provide proof of your answers whenever possible. Speak in a slow non-threatening manner.

*Questions to ask*
- *Why* do you feel that way?
- *Why* is that important to you?
- Do you feel this is the right thing to do?
- Do you feel we can work together on this?

- Can you see *why* this is the right course of action?

*Areas to avoid*
Avoid rushing or cajoling the Amiable customer. Show patience and tolerance and in this way earn their trust and confidence in you. Be firm and friendly, but not insensitive to their feelings.

*Closing the Sale*
Closing the sale with the Amiable requires that you ask for the order. The Amiable buying style is not renowned for its decisiveness. What they will buy is your confidence if you demonstrate it. However, closing statements need to emphasis your need of them as well as the benefits they will gain. For example you might say: *"Can you see why this is the right decision for you?"* Alternatively you might say: *"I am confident that these proposals meet your needs."* Another approach would be: *"Do you see any reason why we should not go ahead right now?"*

If they still procrastinate be prepared to restate the benefits in the form of a close, but do so in a manner that is friendly and warm.

Demonstrating your commitment to the Amiable customer you should be prepared to make further visits, to make the sale and never go back is to the Amiable a betrayal of friendship which in turn appeals to their basic fear.

The whole sales process with an Amiable, then, should be conducted in a friendly and non-threatening manner with the emphasis being placed upon the reasons *Why* they should buy rather than on *How* your product will achieve the objective. This will make the sales process personal rather than abstract and therefore appeal directly to the Amiable's basic desire.

*Organising priorities*
You are inclined to adopt a selling style based upon the following priorities: The *How-What-Why-Who*. To sell to the Amiable customer you need to re-arrange you priorities in the following sequence: The *Why-Who-How-What*. This is very much reflective of their desire to be loved, or needed.

**Snapshot Profile**
- You have a *How* selling style. The Amiable customer has a *Why* buying style (see diagram 8)
- The Amiable's *Basic Desire* - To be loved, needed or valued
- The Amiable's *Basic Fear* - Being unloved unneeded or under-valued (see diagram 9)

## Selling to Expressive customers

As you now know, all personality styles share some common character traits. These areas of commonality allow your natural selling style to converge, to a greater or lesser extent, with customers' buying styles. With the Expressive customer this is still the case but the areas of convergence are extremely limited. For this reason selling to the Expressive customer will present you with your greatest challenge. You will recall that those personality styles diametrically opposed are most alien toward each other. As an Analytical you are diametrically opposed to the Expressive customer. This is because your basic desires differ completely. For you acceptance is a low priority but for the Expressive customer it is pre-eminent (see diagram 9).

Despite being 'opposites' your 'intellectual' approach may seemingly appeal to the Expressive who often likes to consider himself knowledgeable. However, the Expressive will get bored very easily if your assume your natural selling style. So do not be lulled in to thinking they are interested in the *How* of your product, in fact the opposite is more likely to be true (see diagram 8).

*The Sales Presentation*
When dealing with Expressive customers you must retain in the forefront of your mind that their fundamental desire is to be accepted. So long as you are appealing to this basic desire you avoid their basic fear of being rejected. With this in mind you should not be too detached and business-like in your dealings with this type of customer. If possible conduct your sales presentation in a more informal setting, perhaps over a coffee or lunch. It is important also that you do not ask questions related to facts or that are abstract in nature such as; *"Do you see the logic of...?"* The impulse to such questioning should be resisted and the question replaced with one that appeals to their emotions or sense of self i.e. *"Why do you feel that way...?"* Also, solicit their opinions when you can and praise them for their insight or creative solutions offered, particularly when in the company of other people. This again ensures the emphasis is directed toward their basic desire to be accepted.

As already stated, your efficient and business-like manner will make you seem cold and remote to the Expressive customer so it is important you make the effort to be friendly if you are to appeal to their natural buying style. You can achieve this by asking questions that relate to them as individuals rather than as entities. Ask about their work, their recreational activities and in particular their associations.

Once again your pre-packaged solutions or formalised agenda will leave the Expressive no scope to express their individuality which is an essential part of why they buy. The outcome, in terms of a solution to the problem, may be the same but they will want to think it was their idea, so let them and in doing so appeal to their buying style. Secondly, an agenda can be completed other than by going directly from A through to Z. Therefore, modify your selling style by being prepared to let the Expressive customer wander a little. If you should get into areas of disagreement avoid being dogmatic, or analytical in your response. Your rigidity or need to win the 'impersonal' intellectual argument will be interpreted as a personal rejection of them and not their ideas. Such an approach will only appeal to their basic fear of being rejected.

Where you feel the need to substantiate any claims you make about your product try to be selective. Showing the Expressive statistical data will leave them feeling cold no matter how authoritative they may be. Consequently you should keep your description of the product to the high points committing to paper the finer details. You might also try using testimonials from sources or people the Expressive thinks are prominent - the Expressive likes to be associated with the right people.

Your natural efficiency may often mean you allocate the minimum amount of time necessary for each customer you see. If you do this with an Expressive you will undoubtedly run out of time before concluding your business. If you know in advance you are going to see someone who is clearly an Expressive customer allow yourself more time than usual, and use the extra time to relate to them as a person. At the end of the day the Expressive's buying style leads them to buy from the person they like, rather than the one who seems to offer the best deal.

The natural confidence you have in your product knowledge, while giving you authority, may lead you to adopt a superior attitude. This inevitably leaves the Expressive feeling they are being talked down to and this is sure to alienate them as it appeals to a basic fear. As was suggested earlier, let prominent names make your case for you wherever possible by citing customers in the same line of business as them.

As an Analytical your selling style is not given to outward expressions of emotion, but the one emotion you need to cultivate if you want to appeal to the Expressive's buying style is enthusiasm. A dead-pan sales presentation is just dull and boring so far as the Expressive customer is concerned. Get excited and show it. The Expressive will reciprocate in full measure.

*Response guide to questions*
The Expressive customers often much prefers to socialise than talk business. Their questions often reflect a personal desire to be friendly - so reciprocate. Keep factual answers regarding the product simple, if you can get away with a 'Yes' or 'No' answer then do so. They are not overly concerned with proof, or facts and figures so keep them to a bare minimum covering only the high points. Speak with enthusiasm and become animated too.

*Questions to ask*
- Am I right in assuming you will make the final decision?
- Your colleagues will feel the same way I'm sure, don't you agree?
- Based upon your knowledge of the subject which solution do you feel works best?
- I feel I can work with you on this, how do you feel about me?
- Shall I take care of all the necessary paperwork for you?

*Areas to avoid*
Do not allow this type of customer to distract you from the true purpose of your meeting by talking too much. Do not bore them with procedure - just take care of it.

*Closing the Sale*
Having tailored your selling style to appeal to the Expressive nothing will happen when you come to close the sale unless you suggest ideas for implementing action. It is the nature of the Analytical salesperson to rest their case trusting the customer will see the logic of their argument. This approach toward an Expressive customer leaves the whole thing hanging in the air as they would rather talk than do business. At this point the Expressive might even suggest another meeting. Beware of such invites. You are inclined to take such invites as a sign of their serious intention to go away and consider all the facts before buying. However, the Expressive often has no such intention at all. They just want to meet and talk (even more likely if they regard you as a superior intellect). When the time for making a decision arrives either you or the customer has to make a decision and this had better be you if you

don't want to spend your life endlessly talking. To spur the Expressive to action appeal to their buying style by offering an incentive if possible; a special discount for immediate action, or for taking a risk. The Expressive customer's willingness to buy new or innovative products often provides an impetus for immediate action. Such an approach may of course mean you giving up your impulse to offer the tried and tested solution.

Selling to the Expressive will be the greatest test of your versatility. You could avoid the challenge if you like but given Expressives are often influential people ignoring them often means giving up a huge source of potentially influential introductions.

*Organising priorities*
You are inclined to adopt a selling style based upon the following priorities: The *How-What-Why-Who*. To sell to the Expressive customer you need to re-arrange you priorities in the following sequence: The *Who-Why-What-How*. This is very much reflective of the Expressive customers' people orientation as opposed to your fact orientation. It is the former to which you must appeal if you are to win the Expressive customer.

**Snapshot Profile**
- You have a *How* selling style. The Expressive customer has a *Who* buying style (see diagram 8)
- The Expressive's *Basic Desire* - To be accepted
- The Expressive's *Basic Fear* - Being rejected (see diagram 9)

## Selling to fellow Analytical customers

When selling to fellow Analyticals you are in your element. You will come to the meeting with a prepared case, and that will be appreciated by Analytical customers. Your approach will be business-like and focused upon the facts and this will also appeal to the customer's basic desire (see diagram 9). The solid and authoritative evidence used to support your sales presentation will also be appreciated, in fact it may be one of the few occasions when it is. Moreover, it will be scrutinised which doubtless you will appreciate. Most of all though your no-nonsense tried and tested solution to their problems will earn you their respect. Given these areas of commonality it should come as no surprise that this is where you will get your best results. However, whilst you and the customer share the same characteristic virtues you also share the same characteristic vices. For this reason the path to a sale may not be as smooth as you might have initially thought. There will be elements of your selling style likely to clash with the Analytical customers buying style.

*The Sales Presentation*
The basic fear of all Analyticals is that of being overwhelmed by others and no one is more equipped to bring out this basic fear than an Analytical they feel has a 'better' intellect. For this reason bear in mind a few cautionary notes when selling to Analytical customers. Failure to heed these suggestions could mean you end up appealing to the Analytical customers' basic fears, or losing sight of the purpose of the meeting.

The Analytical personality is often characterised as thinking too much and nowhere is too much thinking and not enough action going to occur than when two Analyticals meet. Here lies a danger. There is a high probability that you and the Analytical customer will become fixated on minute details each arguing their case, possibly even becoming aggressive toward each other. Each party will then become preoccupied with defending their own position for fear of being overwhelmed by the other. In such situations each is appealing to the other's basic fear. This situation will persist until eventually the whole purpose of the meeting is lost - finding a solution to the problem.

When two Analyticals engage in such encounters you can also be sure it is going to be a long meeting, often concluding without agreement. This of course serves no purpose, certainly not if one is involved in trying to sell to the other. It is important, therefore that someone, you, remain focused at all times on the overall objective of arriving at a win/win solution.

To achieve this objective you will need to modify your selling style, albeit only slightly, to facilitate the customer's basic desire to understand. This might be aided by both agreeing to, and sticking with, an agreed timetable for reaching a decision. Drawing up an agenda or scheduled approach that leads step-by-step to implementing action is often a very good idea when selling to Analytical customers. This approach appeals directly to their basic desire to understand. In areas where there is agreement move on immediately to the next point. Where disagreements do arise present your case rationally, rather than defend it for the sake of defending it, and lead it toward an outcome rather than becoming bogged down in winning the argument which only appeals to their basic fear. You can aid this process by reinforcing the Analytical customer's basic desire to understand.

Though much of what you do naturally will find favour with the fellow Analytical the guides below might prove useful.

*Response guide to questions*
Analytical customers are cautious and often suspicious individuals. 'Yes' or 'No' answers in response to questions are seldom sufficient. Therefore, you must answer all questions fully, providing documentary evidence whenever possible to support your claims. Speak slowly and in a controlled manner to match the vocal inflexion of the Analytical.

*Questions to ask*
- What are your thoughts on this so far?
- Do you see *how* this will work?
- Would you agree that the evidence is conclusive?
- Can you think of any points we have not covered?
- What conclusions would you draw from this?

*Areas to avoid*
A firm handshake is fine, a slap on the back is not. Avoid getting too familiar or too personal in your questioning. Glib or shallow answers to questions are fatal if you are seeking to build trust and confidence. Avoid last-minute surprises as these are not well received.

*Closing the Sale*

Having concluded your sales presentation it is natural for any Analytical customer to want to consider in detail all the points, this is after all how they like to buy. This inevitably results though is the classic *"Let me think it over"* objection. The problem is compounded though in virtue of you being a fellow Analytical as you are inclined to empathise with the customer at this point. Allowing the objection to stand will necessitate you having to call back which costs you both time and money, and without guarantee of a 'Yes'. To avoid this kind of situation ensure your presentation leads logically to the conclusion that they need to make a definite decision. This might be achieved by saying: *"Based on the evidence I am sure you can see the logic of taking appropriate measures now to resolve this problem."* Alternatively you could say: *"Having considered all the facts in detail within the time allotted I am sure you see the need for immediate counter-measures."*

Whatever phraseology you use it must appeal to their logic, which should be easy for you to do. Remember also that Analytical customers are generally bright people and can grasp very quickly in most instances what is involved and therefore seldom need additional time to consider in more detail your proposals.

*Organising priorities*

You are inclined to adopt a selling style, and the Analytical customer inclined to adopt a buying style, based upon the following priorities: The *How-What-Why-Who*. To sell to the fellow Analytical customer requires no change of emphasis merely a focus upon the customers need to understand and a resolution. Importantly it also requires acknowledgement on your part that you do not have a monopoly on truth.

**Snapshot Profile**
- You have a *How* selling style. The Analytical customer has a *How* buying style (see diagram 8)
- The Analyticals *Basic Desire* - To understand the world around them
- The Analyticals *Basic Fear* - Being threatened or overwhelmed by others (see diagram 9)

# 10 - Modifying your Driver selling style

## Your selling style in brief

As a result orientated individual you have little time for the fine details preferring instead to focus upon the bigger picture and bottom-line issues as they relate to your product. Being a strong minded individualist you are naturally confident and assertive with customers. Given the choice between acting and thinking you much prefer to take action. You relish new challenges and are very much a self-starter.

## Selling to Amiable customers

This 'relator' personality presents you with your greatest challenge requiring you to modify your selling style more with this type of customer than any other. The principle reason is that the Amiable customer's 'relator' style is to be contrasted with your 'loner' style. This makes your selling style diametrically opposed to the Amiable customer's buying style. This is primarily because you basic desires are opposed. For you it is self-reliance, but for the Amiable customer it is a basic desire to be needed (see diagram 9). Despite being 'opposites' paradoxically you both seek to dominate the other, you by power or control, the Amiable customer by emotion (see diagram 1). Despite this seeming shared desire to dominate you will need to modify your selling style which is normally detached to match the Amiable's personable buying style.

*The Sales Presentation*

It is very much your selling style to get to the point quickly with the minimum of frills. This is sure to repel the Amiable customer who wants to get to know you before they buy. To simply proceed with your normal efficient selling style will activate the Amiable's basic fear of not being needed or feeling unloved. Therefore, when encountering an Amiable start your sales presentation with a personal comment; talk about them or something related to them - their family or interests. This will appeal directly to their basic desire of feeling needed. In other words break the ice rather than freeze them out.

Starting your sales presentation with a suitable ice-breaker is probably not going to be too difficult even for the Driver sales personality. However, it is important you continue to relate to the Amiable throughout your presentation if you are to appeal to their buying style and basic desire. This might best be achieved by regularly soliciting their opinions. You may not feel the need to do this as you are probably in total control, but in not doing so you will fail to win over the Amiable who must feel needed. In light of the Amiable's desires it will aid you to structure questions or statements that appeal to them as individuals i.e. *"Tell me, how you feel about this...?" "How do you feel we can solve this problem together?"*

You should also seek areas of common interest with the Amiable customer and be sincere when they open up to you. You should reciprocate by being more open yourself. It is important of course that in being sincere, and in finding areas of common interest, that you do not lose sight of the objective, though admittedly this is seldom a problem Driver's experience, quite the opposite in fact.

Given you have a much higher risk threshold than the Amiable any solution you offer to their needs must be either backed-up with personal assurances, or with maximum guarantees, if you want to appeal to their buying instincts. Also, make your solutions specific, and make them conservative, wherever possible, failing these personal assurances will do.

Beware also that your ability to make quick decisions is not matched by the Amiable and this is likely to cause you frustration. However, it is important that you remain patient while the Amiable deliberates as any signs of frustration only appeals to their basic fear. To minimise frustration on your part it is necessary for you to become more accommodating and understanding. If you are going to appeal to the Amiable customer's basic desire you will also need to draw out their personal aspirations and work with them to show how together you can achieve their goals. Simply employing your dictatorial selling style will only alienate the Amiable customer by making them feel un-valued. So modify your sales presentation to a question asking selling style, and listen to their answers responding to whatever they say with sincerity and understanding. To suddenly assert *"Look! Here's how I see it"*, or, *"Let's stick to the real issues here!"* is sure to drive the Amiable customer into their shell. They will not even try to match your assertiveness, or, more importantly, buy unless you adopt a softer approach that appeals to their basic desire.

When selling to Amiable customers your selling style should also be modified to be delivered slowly, quietly, and in a non-threatening manner. In this way you win the heart of the Amiable and it is their heart you must win before you can win the order. Should disagreements arise watch out for signs of hurt feelings, if you notice any it is important you back-off rather than press your 'advantage'. To press-on would be to disregard their feelings and this again appeals to their basic fear.

From the individual character assessments you will recall that Amiable personalities are not fact and figure orientated in the same way as the Analytical, but they still need data to make a decision. The delivery of such data differs though. With the Amiable regularly check for understanding - they must feel needed. For example you might say: *"Do you have any questions so far Mrs ...?"* Even if they say 'No' watch for possible signs of confusion and should you spot any casually and informally re-present your facts in another way. This might bore you but you have no choice when dealing with this type of customer - they must trust you before they will buy. It is important of course that your selling style is not condescending as the Amiable can spot insincerity a mile off. Even worse, condescension only appeals to their basic fear.

Your natural preoccupation during the sales presentation with *What* the product will provide is alien to the Amiable who wants to know *Why* they should buy, and their reasons are invariably personal. Your emphasis should not therefore be simply bottom-line but tailored to match the personal buying style of the Amiable. So, rather than say, *"What this product will give you is greater margins, flexibility, choice etc."* Instead try *"let me explain why this product is* the *right choice for you...* (give the benefit or reason)."

*Response guide to questions*

The Amiable personality likes things to be taken slowly and wants to be sure that you are trustworthy. Answer their questions fully, while at the same time demonstrating that you genuinely care about them. Provide proof of your answers whenever possible. Speak in a slow non-threatening manner.

*Questions to ask*
- *Why* do you feel that way?
- *Why* is that important to you?
- Do you feel this is the right thing to do?
- Do you feel we can work together on this?
- Can you see *why* this is the right course of action?

*Areas to avoid*
Avoid rushing or cajoling the Amiable customer. Show patience and tolerance and in this way earn their trust and confidence in you. Be firm, friendly, and sensitive to their feelings.

*Closing the Sale*
When it comes to closing the sale do not decide for the Amiable as they will see this as bullying - that basic fear again. You should also avoid offering them various alternative solutions as this is liable to result in procrastination. Instead you can appeal to their buying style by making a joint decision - appeal to the desire to be needed. *"Do you feel, as I do, this product provides us with the best solution?"*

As a Driver servicing customers is not one of your strengths as you would much rather be breaking new ground. Consequently you will often fail to offer any form of personal back-up. This will not endear you to Amiable customers who are relationship orientated and want to develop a working relationship with those whom they do business with. If you do not offer them this opportunity during your sales presentation they are likely to buy from someone who will. If on the other hand you promise a follow-up service, and fail to deliver, you will undermine the possibility of further business. It is important when selling to such customers that you make promises and deliver on them. So be prepared to make additional visits to meet the Amiable to assure them of your genuine interest in them.

*Organising priorities*
You are inclined to adopt a selling style based upon the following priorities: The *What-How-Who-Why*. To sell to the Amiable customer you need to re-arrange you priorities in the following sequence: The *Why-Who-How-What*. This is the opposite of your own selling style hence the type of customer requiring the greatest shift in style. They are emotive personalities who like to feel valued and it is to this desire you must appeal to win the Amiable customer.

**Snapshot Profile**
- You have a *What* selling style. The Amiable customer has a *Why* buying style (see diagram 8)
- The Amiable's *Basic Desire* - To be loved, needed or valued

- The Amiable's *Basic Fear* - Being unloved, unneeded or under-valued (see diagram 9)

## Selling to Expressive customers

As both you and the Expressive customer prefer to deal with new and innovative products you will immediately establish some common ground, but this will be eroded in an instant unless a few basic precautions are taken.

As out-going individuals there will be no shortage of conversation when you meet the Expressive customer. This represents a challenge for while two people can eat, walk, and perhaps even dance at the same time without difficulty, no two people can talk at the same time without problems. As competitive individuals you will both seek to dominate the situation. Given this mutual characteristic someone will need to modify their style if your selling style and the Expressive's buying style are to be in harmony - obviously this should be you. Failure to do so will appeal to their basic fear. Remember, the Expressive's basic desire is it to be accepted, for you it is self-reliance and these are clearly not compatible - one requires people the other doesn't (see diagram 9).

*The Sales Presentation*
While a dialogue is always a possibility between the Driver and Expressive it is imperative you direct it along personal rather than purely business lines as you are inclined to do. The Expressive customer is not task orientated in the same way you are, and you will need to allow the Expressive to express their individuality. Modify your direct selling style by making your presentation a little less business orientated. In this way you will appeal to an Expressive customer's basic desire to be accepted.

In preparing your sales presentation for the Expressive plan interaction and be willing to leave the rigid path between A through to Z. You must be prepared to take detours, perhaps even gossip, particularly about people they regard as prominent. Be prepared also to add statements that support the Expressive's dreams and aspirations. This will help you avoid the mistake of legislating for them and will appeal directly to their basic desire for acceptance. So, it is important you modify your selling style to acknowledge what they desire rather than regarding social niceties as an unwarranted detour from the subject of business. Simple statements along the lines of: *"That's interesting, tell me more"*, are usually sufficient. Another area to avoid is being judgmental as the Expressive customer may regard this as personal rejection - a direct appeal to their basic fear. Remember also that Expressive customers like to be liked and to talk so it is important you listen sincerely and not regard their 'ramblings' as a chore you must endure. There are some real benefits to be gained by appealing to this basic desire.

You might further aid your cause by arranging a meeting in a more informal setting, perhaps over coffee or lunch. If neither of these options is possible then do your utmost to relax them by modifying your direct selling style and breaking preoccupation with business. This, paradoxically, has a more positive outcome on business with the Expressive customers.

You might also relate to the Expressive by asking them for their opinion, or ideas. The Expressive customer will appreciate this, even more so if you complement them on their creativity or insight, and doubly so if other parties are present at the meeting to hear you praise them. However, under no circumstances must you ever criticise an Expressive in the presence of others - they will hate you forever if you do. Their public image is sacred to them and to undermine it is the worst crime you can commit against them. The first approach appeals to their basic desire, the second to their basic fear. Therefore should disagreement arise modify your style and concede a minor point - winning orders is preferable to winning arguments - it is a strange logic to suppose you win orders by winning arguments.

All of this is of course contrary to your own selling style of preferring to stick to the task in hand freed from emotional constraints that 'waste time'. However, it might serve you well to note that the Expressive likes, just as much as you, to move business matters along speedily. In fact the Expressive customer is likely to buy from you with the minimum of presentations, but only if he likes you which requires you to accept him.

Unlike the Analytical you are unlikely to bog down the Expressive with detailed facts, but there is always the danger that you will bore them with whatever you do show or discuss with them. It is important then that you modify your selling style accordingly. Whatever you can put in writing do so and focus the Expressive's mind on differing forms of action they can take to resolve their problem. If you use testimonials use only those highlighting prominent names rather than prominent results as you would normally do. You appeal to an Expressive's buying style by being people orientated, not fact orientated.

*Response guide to questions*

The Expressive customers often much prefers to socialise than talk business. Their questions often reflect a personal desire to be friendly - so reciprocate. Keep factual answers regarding the product simple, if you can get away with a 'Yes' or 'No' answer then do so. They are not overly concerned with proof, or facts and figures so keep them to a bare minimum covering only the high points. Speak with enthusiasm and become animated too.

*Questions to ask*
- Am I right in assuming you will make the final decision?
- Your colleagues will feel the same way I'm sure, don't you agree?
- Based upon your knowledge of the subject which solution do you feel works best?
- I feel I can work with you on this, how do you feel about me?
- Shall I take care of all the necessary paperwork for you?

*Areas to avoid*

Do not allow this type of customer to distract you from the true purpose of your meeting by talking too much. Do not bore them with procedure - just take care of it.

*Closing the Sale*

Offering the Expressive customer new and innovative products will put you on fertile ground when it comes to closing the sale, but beware once again of dictating solutions, i.e. *"This is how I see it"*. It will pay you dividends when closing a sale with an Expressive customer if you acknowledge they dislike personal rejection. They also have the same problem rejecting others. Recognising this character trait enables you to modify your closing style to suit. *"Having had the opportunity to meet and discuss with you this problem I feel good about working with you to solve it. Tell me, how do you feel about working with me?"* This close includes acceptance of them (their basic desire), but also places the emphasis on the relationship, not the product. Alternatively use a close which incorporates a genuine complement, if appropriate: For example *"I can see you are a decisive individual who has managed to grasp this difficult problem with some ease, so let us conclude this matter now and put it to one side."* While these approaches might be too direct to use for other selling styles they are unlikely to present difficulties for the Driver.

Follow-up with the Expressive is also very important so be prepared to go back and see them, even if there is no chance of an immediate further sale. Regard such visits as social calls. They need only be short calls but an investment of time worth making as the Expressive always prefers to buy from those they regard as friends. If you fail to service the Expressive customer they will find another 'friend' and buy from them.

*Organising priorities*
You are inclined to adopt a selling style based upon the following priorities: The *What-How-Who-Why*. To sell to the Expressive customer you need to re-arrange you priorities in the following sequence: The *Who-Why-What-How*. They are relationship-orientated individuals who want to be accepted and you need to appeal to that underlying motivation.

**Snapshot Profile**
- You have a *What* selling style. The Expressive customer has a *Who* buying style (see diagram 8)
- The Expressive's *Basic Desire* - To be accepted
- The Expressive's *Basic Fear* - Being rejected (see diagram 9)

## Selling to Analytical customers

You have as much common ground with Analytical customers as you do with Expressive customers but for different, yet significant, reasons. Neither of you has the desire to develop a relationship beyond what might be described as strictly business. You will relate well, ironically, because neither of you desire the sales process to be anything other than business-like. In this respect your selling style will match the buying style of the Analytical. The upsides of your respective detachment means you can get straight down to business and this will appeal to their basic desire (see diagram 9). Yet getting down to business means different things to the Analytical and the Driver. For the Analytical customer this means weigh and assessing the facts for you, the Driver, it means taking action.

*The Sales Presentation*
While the Analytical will welcome your efficiency they will see your impatience to act as undue haste. To counter this impression you need to modify your selling style to temper all impulses to premature action. It is important for the Analytical to get the facts, all the facts, and not just the points

you deem appropriate. Importantly, given the Analytical customer's thoroughness, you must never be dismissive of the finer detail in favour of the bigger picture. To you these finer points may be just mere detail obscuring the big picture. But, to the Analytical they are vitally important, all of them, as their basic desire is to understand the world around them.

Having resigned yourself to furnishing the Analytical with *all* the relevant data do not simply leave them to peruse them, rather be prepared to go through each one. By contributing in an organised manner to the customer's attempt to understand fully all the implications of his purchase you remain in charge of the sales process. All this requires time of course but there is nothing you can do about that when selling to an Analytical. To do anything less is to be seen to be rushing, and that just will not do. Moreover, pressing them will be treated as an attempt to overwhelm them which only appeals to their basic fear.

Analytical customers tend to be bright, knowing a great deal about their business and how it works, they may even know a great deal about your product, particularly the technical aspects. Such knowledge is unlikely to intimidate you as it might the Amiable or Expressive salesperson, but it will test your patience. You might even find yourself wondering why they can't see *What* the product will do for them. But it must remain a thought because while you are concerned with *What* the product will do, they are concerned with *How* it will do it. So be patient as they must feel they understand what you are offering before they will take any action.

Should areas of disagreement arise resisting the impulse to cajole, coax or bully the Analytical is imperative - again it only appeals to their basic fear. Any such behaviour will be treated with disdain, aside from which they may think you are trying to hide something and become even more cautious than they are already prone to be. Instead modify your selling style so as to present your case in an organised and logical manner, this approach, more than anything else you might have to say, will appeal to their basic desire and buying style.

While one of your main characteristics is a willingness to take risks this is not matched by the Analytical, so be warned. During your sales presentation do not even hint that they should 'take a gamble'. Before doing anything so rash as buying the Analytical customer will want solid, practical and authoritative evidence that your proposal will work, so this means you must focus on the tried and tested solutions rather than the innovative. They will also want guarantees, not personal assurances, and they certainly do not regard some third party opinion as evidence, so do not offer it.

Any testimonials you might have to offer about your product will appeal to the Analytical as they will principally be authoritative, but make sure they are not too selective or out of date, the analytical will spot both. If they feel you have been selective in your choice of data or testimonials the Analytical customer will want to make further enquiries. Likewise, if they feel that your information is out of date they will search out more recent data. Gathering all this extra information will take time, time you generally can't spare, and you can avoid this 'time wasting' by supplying them with up-to-date data - still hot from the press preferably.

Analytical customers are nature's procrastinators so you should try to establish a decision-making time schedule. You can do this by getting them to work to an agreed timetable or agenda that has been agreed in advance of the meeting. This timetable should be a logical, step-by-step process leading to a resolution/conclusion within the timeframe agreed.

*Response guide to questions*

Analytical customers are cautious and often suspicious individuals. 'Yes' or 'No' answers in response to questions are seldom sufficient. Therefore, you must answer all questions fully, providing documentary evidence whenever possible to support your claims. Speak slowly and in a controlled manner to match the vocal inflexion of the Analytical.

*Questions to ask*
- What are your thoughts on this so far?
- Do you see *how* this will work?
- Would you agree that the evidence is conclusive?
- Can you think of any points we have not covered?
- What conclusions would you draw from this?

*Areas to avoid*

A firm handshake is acceptable but a slap on the back is not. Avoid getting too familiar or too personal in your questioning. Glib or shallow answers to questions raised are fatal if you are seeking to build trust and confidence. Avoid last-minute surprises as these are not well received.

*Closing the Sale*

Your natural selling style is characterised by an eagerness to get a quick decision. This will be perceived by the Analytical customer as either bullying or a desire to hide some relevant facts. This approach will only appeal to their fear of being dominated by another and therefore sure to alienate them. Instead modify your appeal to their desire to understand by giving them the time agreed on in advance in which to make their decision. When sufficient time has been allowed for them to weigh-up the facts your close should reflect *their* desire to be in control: This might be achieved by saying: "*Having had time to consider all the facts which solution do you believe best solves the problem?*" Note that this closing question makes reference to facts not feelings, it is not personal but problem centred, and finally, it puts the final decision in their hands. Any decision the Analytical customer makes must of course be their decision. Moreover, this approach deals in the abstract not the personal, and your selling style should always be mindful of this fact.

*Organising priorities*

You are inclined to adopt a selling style based upon the following priorities: The *What-How-Who-Why*. To sell to the Analytical customer you need to re-arrange your priorities in the following sequence: The *How-What-Why-Who*. The main emphasis here is on the distinction between the *How* and the *What* with the rest all a poor second consideration. So state facts before you state the benefits of your product as this will help them to understand.

**Snapshot Profile**
- You have a *What* selling style. The Analytical customer has a *How* buying style (see diagram 8)
- The Analyticals *Basic Desire* - To understand the world around them
- The Analyticals *Basic Fear* - Being threatened or overwhelmed by others (see diagram 9)

## Selling to fellow Driver customers

Selling to a like-minded person your natural selling style places you in a favourable position with Driver customers. You will be to the point and business-like. Your prepared 'package' will be presented in an organised manner with attention given only to the salient points, in particular, *What* your product will do for them. Recognising the need for your fellow Driver to make up his own mind you will present them with alternatives from which they can chose; alternatives that emphasis results or attainment of objectives. This will appeal to their basic desire for self-reliance (see diagram 9).

Given all these 'advantages' you may be forgiven for thinking you should just sell to Driver customers. But even supposing you could qualify (i.e. know enough) your customers sufficiently well in advance I am afraid that life is seldom that simple. Aside from which it will not be all plain sailing as you might have thought. This is because while you share the same characteristic virtues you also share the same characteristic vices, and this is where you may encounter difficulties. For this reason a few cautionary notes are worth attending to.

*The Sales Presentation*
Your recognition of a fellow Driver's desire to be self-reliant is matched by your respective fear of submitting to the will of others. Therefore, your characteristic temptation during the sales presentation to control could result in a battle of wills that will ultimately result in a lose/lose outcome. You therefore need to avoid dominating the Driver customer because this appeals directly to their basic fear of being controlled. To avoid such outcomes you need to transcend this basic temptation to control and modify your selling style to match that particular Driver's buying style. This does not mean of course you taking the subservient role - 'submitting' just to get the sale. Rather it requires you to re-assert yourself differently. That is to say in a manner that emphasises your virtues, not your vices.

You will recall that when outlining the characteristic virtues of Drivers that an outgrowth of possession and control was magnanimity. This is a selfless quality whereby you exercise control over your own basic desires, not another person. In recognising you cannot control everyone or everything you will be able to modify your selling style so as to reassert yourself in a more balanced manner. In other words, avoid appealing to your basic desire but rather to the customer's basic desire for self-reliance. As a consequence of such an approach you use leadership rather than raw power which results in the other party turning to you for direction and guidance. Rather than a battle of wills occurring when two Drivers meet you instead earn the respect of the Driver customer for being forthright and honourable. In other words, you need to modify your selling style so that you exercise your will constructively rather than merely to control. The balanced Driver salesperson, then, is one who, in relinquishing their desire to dominate, becomes less concerned with self-interest and more interested in the welfare and interests of their customer. In truth, the only way to sell to a fellow driver is to appeal to their basic desire for self-reliance.

Though much of what you do naturally will find favour with the fellow Driver the guides below might prove useful.

*Response guide to questions*
The Driver wants you to get to the point quickly and does not want long-winded answers to their questions, 'Yes' and 'No' answers are often sufficient. They want you to be business-like, efficient and brief. Stick to the main features of your product or bottom-line results. Speak with confidence and authority.

*Questions to ask*
- How do you feel you can best achieve your objectives?
- *What* have you done about them so far?
- Which option do you believe best achieves your objective?
- Is this agreed?
- When do you want it by?

*Areas to avoid*
Do not be indecisive when dealing with this type of person, they want you to provide them with answers, not problems. Inefficiency is not looked upon favourably so do what you say you will, or do not offer at all. Do not bore them with details take care of them yourself whenever possible.

*Closing the Sale*
Your natural selling style is characterised by an eagerness to get a quick decision. The Driver will always give you a quick decision and seldom requires time to consider the issue at length. Whether or not they give you the right decision will depend on how well you have managed them. The best approach when closing a Driver customer is to simply ask for a decision there and then. This will appeal to their basic desire for self-reliance.

*Organising priorities*
You are inclined to adopt a selling style, and the Driver customer inclined to adopt a buying style, based on the following priorities: The *What-How-Who-Why*. To sell to the fellow Driver customer requires no change in emphasis merely a re-assertion of your will to bring about a win/win outcome by appealing to their basic desire.

**Snapshot Profile**
- You have a *What* selling style. The Driver customer has a *What* buying style (see diagram 8)
- The Driver's *Basic Desire* - Self-reliance
- The Driver's *Basic Fear* - Submitting to the will of others (see diagram 9)

# 11 - Modifying your Amiable selling style

## Your selling style in brief

As an empathetic person you have compassion and feeling for others. You are concerned about the needs of others often adopting a parenting role. Service is important and you will go out of your way to give the customer what they need. In ensuring you meet the customer's needs you will take time with them to explain the facts, and do so in a non-threatening manner. You are a patient individual prepared to invest time in others.

## Selling to Expressive customers

Both you and the Expressive customer are distinguishable by your genuine concern for others. This feeling for others allows you to reveal your true personality. Consequently your openness, friendliness, helpfulness and supportive nature will endear you to Expressive customer. However, while your basic desire is to be loved the Expressive customer desires only to be accepted, therefore they might find your intimacy a little too intense. You must therefore modify your selling style only to show you accept them (see diagram 9).

*The Sales Presentation*

As both you and the Expressive customer are emotive personalities it is unlikely you will activate the Expressive's basic fear of being rejected and in all probability you will, for the most part, appeal to their basic desire to be accepted. But that does not mean your sales presentation will be plain sailing for there are a number of high risk areas which could be a source of alienation.

You may find the customer with an Expressive personality a little brash or loud and this may be intimidating. This is not something you need be overly concerned about given the customer only wants you to like them.

You selling style may also be a little on the reserved side for the average Expressive who is much more outgoing and fun loving. You will therefore need to add spice to your sales presentation, not to mention a little more pace and enthusiasm in its delivery. You also tend to be cautious in your approach to solutions and the Expressive customer may find this a little dull. The Expressive customer likes the unusual and innovative whereas you like the tried and tested. So, it would pay you to be a little more creative in your choice of solution if this is possible. Failing this, sell what you have got with plenty of enthusiasm.

While you have a low risk threshold it must be remembered that the Expressive customer has a much higher tolerance for risk. What you might regard as too risky the Expressive will not, so appeal to their buying instincts by upping the stakes a little. Importantly, then, when selling to Expressive customers relax your normal reserve and present them with high reward/risk solutions to problems - the Expressive likes to be recognised for daring. Again this is all part of their desire for acceptance so acknowledge the Expressive's achievements.

Your natural caution also leads you to believe it is important that the customer knows all the minute details of the product. This is not so for the Expressive customer so be prepared to modify your selling style to exclude the finer details of your product. In fact, whenever possible commit to paper as many of the finer details as is possible. Selling the main features or high points of your product is not only preferred by the Expressive customer but will appeal to the their buying style. At the end of the day the expressive is more interested in *Who* else has bought the product, rather than *Why* they should buy it.

The concern the Expressive has with other people is something you should take notice of in other areas of the sales process. Do not talk solely to your customer about them but ask about other people they might know. Secondly, when presenting testimonials, or other authoritative evidence, try to select those which highlight people or organisations the Expressive is likely to deem prominent - the signatory or letter-headed paper is often more important to the Expressive than what they attest to.

Whilst you will be sympathetic toward the Expressive customer avoid the temptation of being judgmental (*Characteristic vices*, chapter 4). However, do not avoid praising altogether, if the Expressive customer offers any ideas praise them, especially if in the company of a third party. In fact solicit their ideas as often as you can. The Expressive is a creative individual who may well contribute something worthwhile to the discussion. Moreover, praise and recognition equates to acceptance and so appeals to their basic desire.

*Response guide to questions*

The Expressive customers often much prefers to socialise than talk business. Their questions often reflect a personal desire to be friendly - so reciprocate. Keep factual answers regarding the product simple, if you can get away with a 'Yes' or 'No' answer then do so. They are not overly concerned with proof, or facts and figures so keep them to a bare minimum covering only the high points. Speak with enthusiasm and become animated.

*Questions to ask*
- Am I right in assuming you will make the final decision?
- Your colleagues will feel the same way I'm sure, don't you agree?
- Based upon your knowledge of the subject which solution do you feel works best?
- I feel I can work with you on this, how do you feel about me?
- Shall I take care of all the necessary paperwork for you?

*Areas to avoid*

Do not allow this type of customer to distract you from the true purpose of your meeting by talking too much. Do not bore them with procedure - just take care of it.

*Closing the Sale*

Your natural reserve and low risk threshold could potentially pose problems when closing the sale with an Expressive customer. These natural cautions can make you seem indecisive at the point of closing the sale. When matched with the Expressive's indecisiveness there is always the possibility both you and the customer will end up 'thinking about it' rather than taking action. To overcome this problem modify your selling style to include alternatives from which the Expressive can choose, e.g. *"I can see you are a decisive individual so which option shall we go for?"* Offering alternatives will also make you appear more decisive. If there is a special incentive you can offer to the customer for a quick decision or for taking a higher risk offer this also.

Follow-up service is something that comes naturally to you but make the visit includes a social element as this equates to acceptance of them. It might also help if you arrange meetings in an informal setting - so offer to buy them lunch or coffee. However, never spend too long with the Expressive as they get bored quickly and usually have much to do. Better they are disappointed at you having to leave early, than disappointed because you stayed too long.

*Organising priorities*
You are inclined to adopt a selling style based upon the following priorities: The *Why-Who-How-What*. To sell to the Expressive customer you need to re-arrange you priorities in the following sequence the *Who-Why-What-How*. In doing so your selling style is directed toward their basic desire to be accepted.

**Snapshot Profile**
- You have a *Why* selling style. The Expressive customer has a *Who* buying style (see diagram 8)
- The Expressive's *Basic Desire* - To be accepted
- The Expressive's *Basic Fear* - Being rejected (see diagram 9)

## Selling to Analytical customers

The Analytical customer does not offer you your greatest challenge, this is yet to come, but nonetheless they remain a major challenge for the Amiable salesperson. This is because for you emotion rules, whereas for the Analytical customer intellect rules. Your challenge, then, is to restrain your emotions and become more objective in your selling style. This shifts the balance of your sales presentation away from your basic desire to be needed and toward the Analytical customer's basic desire to understand the world around them (see diagram 9). This having been said there should be enough common ground between you and the Analytical customer to be able to establish a working relationship. For example your respective attitudes toward both change and risk are similar, so is your preference for the tried and tested product or solution. Your lack of assertiveness in comparison with say a Driver personality is also a plus point on your side when dealing with Analytical customers. Another trait that your natural selling style will bring to the fore is your natural caution - your need to weigh-up the evidence. So much seems to be on your side when selling to this type of customer, but potential problems are likely to occur unless you modify your selling style.

*The Sales Presentation*
For you it is important to get to know the other person well and to this end you will ask lots of personal questions. This approach will not, however, be well received by the Analytical customer who will regard such intrusions as wholly irrelevant to the issues in hand. Therefore, you need to modify

your selling style so that it is delivered in a detached manner dealing only with the facts and not the person. You can achieve this by asking questions or making statements that focus upon the *How* rather than the *Why* of the product. For example, *"This is how it is achieved..."* As opposed to, *"Why we need to achieve this is..."* Here you can see the emphasis is made on their main organising priority, and not yours and so appeals to their buying style, not your preferred selling style.

With detachment still in mind do not make personal appeals to the Analytical customer such as: *"I can assure you."* or, *"Trust me."* That which is personally underwritten means nothing to the Analytical. They want the facts not you to support the case. This again highlights the basic difference in your underlying desires. So offering personal assurances will not help your credibility with the Analytical. What will help will be you 'knowing your stuff'. The Analytical is avaricious for knowledge and if they think you know what you are talking about they will not only be eager to learn from you, but also be more respectful of you. Remember therefore to appeal to their basic desire to understand and suppress your desire to be needed.

Your easy-going approach may also lead you into other difficulties with the Analytical. It is vitally important that you make sure your case is well prepared in advance and presented professionally. This means not turning up to the meeting with hand-written proposals or crumpled papers. Your 'home-made' casual approach will be looked upon with disdain by the well-organised Analytical.

Where areas of potential disagreement arise between you and the customer avoid becoming emotionally defensive. It is important when dealing with Analytical customers that you stick rigidly to the facts and make an organised presentation of your position. Emotions, as far as the Analytical are concerned, have nothing to do with the process in hand. Such detachment can be intimidating but if you know your facts and present your case firmly and with confidence this will go a long way to getting the outcome you want with the Analytical customer. Also do not lose confidence because of their challenges or scepticism.

*Response guide to questions*

Analytical customers are cautious and often suspicious individuals. 'Yes' or 'No' answers in response to questions are seldom sufficient. Therefore, you must answer all questions fully, providing documentary evidence whenever possible to support your claims. Speak slowly and in a controlled manner to match the vocal inflexion of the Analytical.

*Questions to ask*
- What are your thoughts on this so far?
- Do you see *how* this will work?
- Would you agree that the evidence is conclusive?
- Can you think of any points we have not covered?
- What conclusions would you draw from this?

*Areas to avoid*

A firm handshake is fine, a slap on the back is not. Avoid getting too familiar or too personal in your questioning. Glib or shallow answers to questions raised are fatal if you are seeking to build trust and confidence. Avoid last-minute surprises as these are not well received.

*Closing the Sale*

From the character descriptions already given you know the Analytical is not an assertive individual, but they can be domineering. For this reason you should shield the softer side of your personality as they will regard this as a sign of weakness and adopt the dominant role. This can be particularly problematic for you when it comes to closing the sale as their perceived 'superior' knowledge may intimidate you to the extent that you may not even attempt to close the sale. To overcome this potential loss of control use logic, a step-by-step approach that leads directly to action within an agreed timetable - the implementation of 'the plan'. In fact this will be helpful as neither you, nor the Analytical, are renowned for speedy action both preferring instead to contemplate and weigh-up the facts. To ensure a decision is reached you might say: "*Having now considered all the facts which option do you believe provides the best solution...?*" Whilst you will always be willing to make further visits to see the undecided Analytical be sure agreement is reached as to when a decision will be made - without this agreement the sales process could run on, and on, and on. This will do neither of you any good.

*Organising priorities*

You are inclined to adopt a selling style based upon the following priorities: The *Why-Who-How-What*. To sell to the Analytical customer you need to re-arrange your priorities in the following sequence: The *How-What-Why-Who*. In doing so you will appeal to their basic need to know. More importantly you will avoid the error of turning what the Analytical regards as an objective process of decision making in to a subjective one. In other words, keep the emphasis on their desire to understand and not your desire to be needed.

**Snapshot Profile**
- You have a *Why* selling style. The Analytical customer has a *How* buying style (see diagram 8)
- The Analyticals *Basic Desire* - To understand the world around them
- The Analyticals *Basic Fear* - Being threatened or overwhelmed by others (see diagram 9)

# Selling to Driver customers

The Driver customer presents you with your greatest challenge. You are 'opposites' in all respects, diametrically opposed, and therefore almost everything you do naturally in the sales process is likely to be alien to them. This is principally because your basic desire and their basic desire clash. For the Driver self-reliance is pre-eminent, however, your basic desire is to be needed (see diagram 9). For this reason you need to modify your selling style more with this type of customer than any other. Modifying your selling style to match the Driver customer's buying style will, then, be a true test of your versatility. However, those aspects of your natural selling style the Driver customer will appreciate, few as they are, will be you overall helpfulness and supportive nature.

*The Sales Presentation*

Despite being opposites paradoxically you both seek to dominate others, you by emotion, the Driver by control (see diagram 1). It is important then that you temper your desire to introduce the personal, or emotional, into the sales presentation and instead stick strictly to business matters. This will help you to keep your mind off your desire and on the Driver's.

Another potential problem area with this sort of customer is your basic friendliness. For you it is important to get to know the customer personally. The Driver however neither needs to know you nor sees the need for you to know them. They can conduct business at arm's length if you like, so to avoid engaging in what they will regard as prattle modify your selling style so that you get straight down to business. In short, while you may feel the need to be needed, they simply don't share your basic desire as self-reliance is their primary motivator. However, sticking to the issues involves more than avoiding personal questions with the Driver. When selling to the Driver you should also avoid any questions not relating directly to the big picture, the major problem or objective.

You might best achieve the focus necessary for dealing with the Driver by preparing your sales presentation well in advance. Where possible rehearse your presentation in advance eliminating all 'secondary' material and that which remains organise into a 'package', but be careful not to come to the meeting with a ready-made solution. I will give more guidance on this momentarily. The emphasis when dealing with Driver customers is: be clear, be specific, and, preferably, be brief. If your particular sales presentation lends itself to the use of an agenda then this might also help you make the style modifications necessary. It will help you to keep on track and the customer to know when your presentation will end. If the use of an agenda is not possible then outline in advance the points you will be covering during your sales presentation.

Presenting your case in the manner outlined will also help avoid gaps or loopholes in your presentation which, if the Driver spots them, will be attacked aggressively. Remember, the Driver is a forceful character that 'takes no prisoners', so be prepared. It is important however, their 'aggressive' responses not be interpreted as a rejection of you, that you are not needed. Rather it is simply an assertion of their basic desire for self-reliance.

Any questions asked of the Driver personality should preferably be *What* questions as this is the first of their organising principles. For example, *"What is your objective?"*. Alternatively, *"What do you think is the major obstacle?"* Perhaps even, *"What solution do you believe is best?"* As stated in the previous case study, avoid *Why* questions, this is your organising priority, not theirs.

You will of course have few, if any, problem in providing the Driver with facts and figures as this comes naturally to you, but your emphasis needs to be re-focused on the customer's buying style. This should be either the probability of success, or effectiveness of options. Be mindful however of dwelling on minute details. The Driver does not need to know everything about your product only the main features or bottom-line and can usually make their decision on those alone, or will delegate the 'minor' details to a subordinate. Should disagreement occur over facts it is important you avoid the temptation to give either personal assurances, or the temptation to agree in order to appease them. If you know your facts then back them up with confidence and when agreement is reached support the results or facts, not the person. The key to motivating the Driver to take positive action is by referring directly to objectives and results and how *they* might achieve them.

Your natural caution tends to make you conservative when it comes to offering solutions, but the Driver will regard this as 'small thinking' and simply loose interest. You need therefore to be braver and think big in order to grab the Driver's attention. You must also resist the temptation to offer tried and tested solutions as the Driver's buying instinct is toward the innovative, so cater to that impulse.

*Response guide to questions*
The Driver wants you to get to the point quickly and does not want long-winded answers to their questions, 'Yes' and 'No' answers are often sufficient. They want you to be business-like, efficient and brief. Stick to the main features of your product or bottom-line results. Speak with confidence and authority.

*Questions to ask*
- How do you feel you can best achieve your objectives?
- *What* have you done about them so far?
- Which option do you believe best achieves your objective?
- Is this agreed?
- When do you want it by?

*Areas to avoid*
Do not be indecisive when dealing with this type of person, they want you to provide them with answers, not problems. Inefficiency is not looked upon favourably so do what you say you will, or do not offer at all. Do not bore them with details take care of them yourself whenever possible.

*Closing the Sale*
You will need to be bold and take the initiative at the point of closing the sale for any lack of confidence exhibited will be seized upon by the Driver who is always looking to take control. Acknowledge at the same time the need for the Driver to make their own decision. To achieve this double objective, of taking the initiative and letting them decide, give a simple alternative close. For example, *"Having examined the options presented which do you now think best enables you to achieve your objective ...?"* Support whatever option they choose and go straight to the order form. There is no room for timidity when closing with Drivers.

To ensure that a solid foundation is established for future business do not, once the sale has been made, slip into your normal selling style and get personal. Once the deal is done leave promptly afterwards. Friendly chat is something for which the Driver has little tolerance.

*Organising priorities*
You are inclined to adopt a selling style based upon the following priorities: The *Why-Who-How-What*. To sell to the Driver customer you need to re-arrange your priorities in the following,

reverse, sequence: The *What-How-Who-Why*. They are Control orientated individuals who Tell and you are an Emotive orientated personality that Asks (see diagram 1). This need to control is a manifestation of their basic desire for self-reliance and it is important therefore that you appeal to this instinct.

**Snapshot Profile**
- You have a *Why* selling style. The Driver customer has a *What* buying style (see diagram 8)
- The Driver's *Basic Desire* - Self-reliance
- The Driver's *Basic Fear* - Submitting to the will of others (see diagram 9)

## Selling to fellow Amiable customers

You might feel no guidance is required when selling to kindred spirits. Your intuition is right here, but not wholly. On the positive side your selling style will appeal directly to the Amiable customer's need to get to know you, so you will not rush straight down to business. You will also naturally sell in a style that takes the personal and emotive detours necessary to build mutual trust. This will appeal to their basic desire to be needed (see diagram 9). There will be no skimping on the factual detail of your product which will further endear you to the Amiable customer. Yet despite this natural rapport problem areas can still arise and it is important these are addressed if you are to maximise what is, after all, your natural market.

*The Sales Presentation*

The first of the potential problems centres on the Amiable customer's basic desire to be needed. Fulfilling this need is not always easily achieved as you share the basic desire. The unaware Amiable salesperson can fall into the trap of talking more about their own feelings than those of the customer. To satisfy the customer's needs requires a modification of selling style to place emphasis on their feelings. Failure to shift the emphasis could result in no real dialogue taking place, but rather two monologues where each person attempts to satisfy their own basic desire. Avoiding this dual-monologue syndrome requires you to listen and become *customer-centred*. This can be achieved by modifying your selling style to include support statements and *Why* questioning. For example, "*Why do you feel that way?*" As opposed to saying, "*You know, I had a similar experience once..*" This latter response would clearly be a *self-centred* response. If the Amiable customer feels their needs are not being met they can become resentful. This is not the kind of feeling you want to invoke in an Amiable customer, principally as it appeals to their basic fear of being unneeded.

Another area likely to cause problems is the failure to recognise that not all Amiable customers are alike. Some Amiable's are more open than others so it is important you tread gently to begin with, rather than presuming your natural selling style will carry the day. To be too solicitous or intrusive in your questioning could be disturbing for customers who are less open.

Though much of what you do naturally will find favour with the fellow Amiable the guides below might prove useful.

*Response guide to questions*

The Amiable personality likes things to be taken slowly and wants to be sure that you are trustworthy. Answer their questions fully, while at the same time demonstrating that you genuinely care about them. Provide proof of your answers whenever possible. Speak in a slow non-threatening manner.

*Questions to ask*
- *Why* do you feel that way?
- *Why* is that important to you?
- Do you feel this is the right thing to do?
- Do you feel we can work together on this?
- Can you see *why* this is the right course of action?

*Areas to avoid*
Avoid rushing or cajoling the Amiable customer. Show patience and tolerance and in this way earn their trust and confidence in you. Be firm and friendly, but not insensitive to their feelings.

*Closing the Sale*
The potential dangers I have described for the Amiable salesperson are not of course typical as most are able to maintain a sense of balance having enough genuine empathy to identify with others and therefore can act as a catalyst for win/win outcomes. But a problem that is typical, even among 'healthy' Amiables, which needs to be addressed is the tendency of the Amiable to let the other person decide appropriate courses of action. This is most likely to occur at the point of sale resulting in both parties 'Thinking about it' because neither is prepared to take the initiative. To avoid this you need to modify your selling style to exhibit a more direct approach to decision making - to be more confident. If you are confident it is likely your fellow Amiable will buy some of that confidence. Importantly though this self-assurance should not exclude recognition of the Amiable customer's basic desire to feel needed. Be mindful therefore of not overriding this need and in the process appealing to their basic fear of feeling unwanted, or unloved.

*Organising priorities*
You are inclined to adopt a selling style, and the Amiable customer inclined to adopt a buying style, based upon the following priorities: The *Why-Who-How-What*. To sell to the fellow Amiable customer requires no change in emphasis merely a need for you to act as both a confidant and exude confidence in outlining an appropriate course of action.

**Snapshot Profile**
- You have a *Why* selling style. The Amiable customer has a *Why* buying style (see diagram 8)
- The Amiable's *Basic Desire* – To be loved, needed or valued
- The Amiable's *Basic Fear* – Being unloved, unneeded or under-valued (see diagram 9)

# 12 - Modifying your Expressive selling style

## Your selling style in brief

As an individual you are self-assured, confident and have high self-esteem. The description of you as being a 'socialiser' is apt as you enjoy the company of customers and therefore relish the opportunity to meet with them. Given your self-confidence you are a naturally good communicator at ease with a wide variety of people. Competition and status are two key elements in your life, so you not only like to do well, but also be seen to be doing well. Facts and figures bore you.

## Selling to Analytical customers

Despite being described as 'opposites' there does exist some area of common ground upon which you and the Analytical customer can build. The Analytical is a similarly imaginative person and therefore may well respond to your thought provoking ideas and vivid imagination. Yet once having stimulated the Analytical customer's imagination you then begin to drift apart. This is principally because you both desire different things. The Analytical customer is motivated by a basic desire to understand the world around them. On the other hand your basic desire is to be accepted (see diagram 9). Not only do you differ markedly in your underlying motivations, but everything else that comes naturally to you will be alien to the Analytical. Therefore, if you are going to make any progress with Analytical customers you must be prepared to exercise your versatility to the full.

*The Sales Presentation*

The areas where you will need to modify your selling style are numerous. To begin with, your outward display of confidence will disturb the Analytical who is a naturally quiet and cautious person. Their description of you, if asked, might contain some uncomplimentary adjectives such as brash, opinionated, loud and emotional, in fact, all the things they themselves are not. To avoid alienating the Analytical you need to modify your selling style so that your approach is more measured, direct and straightforward in manner. This requires you stick strictly to business. This will shift the balance of the presentation away from your desire to be accepted in favour of their desire to understand. You should not however attempt to impress the Analytical with what you know. Rather let them discover for themselves what you know. The Analytical will have more confidence in discovering this fact than if you simply tell them. Again, this shifts the emphasis from your basic desire to theirs.

You should also avoid the informalities characteristic of your natural selling style, and not be vague on any point the Analytical customer raises. If you do not know the answer to a question asked by the Analytical make a note of it, written preferably, and say you will get back to them. This does not always mean you will need to do so as it might be a minor point, but it will help with establishing your credibility in the eyes of the Analytical.

Planning your sales presentation in advance will be extremely helpful to both you and the Analytical customer. The use of an agenda will aid you in modifying your selling by giving you a track to run on. More importantly it ensures the emphasis is on their desires, not yours. An agenda will also help the Analytical by letting them know in advance what is coming - they hate surprises. Having set the agenda, or at the very least outlined to them verbally the format the meeting will take, resist the temptation to rush through it. Complete each stage logically before moving on to the next item. You need to be patient with the Analytical who likes to weigh-up all the implications. Be prepared therefore for lots of questions that you will need to answer fully. You cannot use your charm on the Analytical to gloss over the details. Accepting the maxim that you have to 'go along to get along' will help immeasurable in improving your appeal to the Analytical.

Should disagreement arise it is unlikely you will whimper in the face of a 'superior' intellect, but you might take such disagreements personally. However, there is no point in taking things personally as the Analytical does not deal in emotions, only facts, and any dispute is simply disagreement about the facts, not about you. Bearing this in mind it is important you make an organised presentation focusing on the facts about your product. Where agreement is found confirm it and move on to the next point.

The use of testimonials is highly recommended with Analytical customers but you might need to re-arrange your portfolio as it is likely it will be littered with those that highlight names of people or organisations you deem prominent. This is unlikely to impress the Analytical who has little respect for anything other than sources they deem authoritative, i.e. fellow Analytical sources. Neither will a flashing glimpse of these testimonials be enough to satisfy the Analytical, so be prepared for them to read each one. Other forms of evidence you might use to support your case must also be solid and reliable, someone else's opinion, including your own, is not evidence for the Analytical so do not use them. For the Analytical customer facts are to be relied upon, not people. Should you find your evidence to be out of date you can almost guarantee the Analytical will spot this and ask for the latest data before taking any action - so make sure your evidence is both current and relevant.

Being a natural risk taker your natural selling style is to offer solutions that are innovative or speculative. Temper this impulse when dealing with the Analytical who much prefers the tried and tested. Where you can offer guarantees with your product do so and be sure they are solid, if anyone will read the small print of a contract it will be an Analytical. Avoid at all times offering your personal assurances to the Analytical. If it is not written down it means little to them.

*Response guide to questions*

Analytical customers are cautious and often suspicious individuals. 'Yes' or 'No' answers in response to questions are seldom sufficient. Therefore, you must answer all questions fully, providing documentary evidence whenever possible to support your claims. Speak slowly and in a controlled manner to match the vocal inflexion of the Analytical.

*Questions to ask*
- What are your thoughts on this so far?
- Do you see *how* this will work?
- Would you agree that the evidence is conclusive?
- Can you think of any points we have not covered?

- What conclusions would you draw from this?

*Areas to avoid*
A firm handshake is acceptable but a slap on the back is not. Avoid getting too familiar or too personal in your questioning. Glib or shallow answers to questions raised are fatal if you are seeking to build trust and confidence. Avoid last-minute surprises as these are not well received.

*Closing the Sale*
If you have used an agenda for the meeting, even if roughly outlined, and if you have not rushed through it, then the Analytical customer will be with you when you get to the end of your presentation. You are then ideally placed to close the sale which would be helped considerably if your agenda included a timetable for making the decision. If not you can add to the verbally outlined agenda a statement along the following lines: *"Having completed the above process you will then have all the information necessary upon which to base your decision. At this point I am sure you will be able to judge for yourself the appropriate course of action."* Alternatively, and more simply: *"Having studied all the facts you will then be in a position to decide."* When you then get to the end of your sales presentation you need only to say: *"As was agreed at the outset. Having studied all the facts you will be in a position to decide. Tell me, which option do you feel provides the best solution...?"* Be warned though, the Analytical is not renowned for making quick decisions and you should be prepared to go back, with more data if necessary. The important thing to remember in closing the Analytical is not to cajole them. This only appeals to their basic fear. Instead place the emphasis on control and their desire to understand.

*Organising priorities*
You are inclined to adopt a selling style based upon the following priorities: The *Who-Why-What-How*. To sell to the Analytical customer you need to re-arrange you priorities in the following sequence: The *How-What-Why-Who*. This is very much reflective of their fact, as opposed to your people, orientation. It is imperative when selling to the Analytical that the emphasis remains on the facts.

**Snapshot Profile**
- You have a *Who* selling style. The Analytical customer has a *How* buying style (see diagram 8)
- The Analyticals *Basic Desire* - To understand the world around them
- The Analyticals *Basic Fear* - Being threatened or overwhelmed by others (see diagram 9)

## Selling to Driver customers

Both you and the Driver customer are competitive and ambitious individuals and consequently have something in common. Similarly your preference and enthusiasm for the new and innovative will be well received when dealing with the Driver customer. There are however despite these similarities, some major differences between your selling style and the Driver's buying style. For you it is important to be accepted and therefore you are inclined to be personable, which means asking personal questions

However, the Driver has no particular need to be liked, or a need to like you for that matter, in order to buy from you. This emphasis by the customer reflects their basic desire for self-reliance (see diagram 9). For this reason you will need to modify your selling style in order to shift the emphasis away from your desire to be accepted and toward their desire for self-reliance.

*The Sales Presentation*

Given the Driver's single-mindedness it pays to get straight to the point and not, as the Driver sees it, 'ramble on about all and sundry', they hate to waste time. Therefore modify your selling style so that what you say is clear, specific, and brief. Importantly, you must convince them you can deliver what you say you can.

To aid your effectiveness come to the sales meeting fully prepared, do not fumble around or look disorganised or the Driver will start clock watching and become impatient with you. Come with a prepared 'package' and highlight all the high points, or main features of your product, emphasising *What* they will achieve for them. This emphasis on the main features of your product should come naturally to you as you also have little time for the minute details. Be careful though not to leave any loopholes in your case as the Driver will spot them and destroy your whole presentation, remember, they like to control and will seize any opportunity to do so.

Having prepared your sales presentation ensure it remains focused and does not distract the Driver's attention from business, avoid asking rhetorical questions or indeed any 'useless' ones. Remember it is their basic desire you need to satisfy, not your own. Any questions asked should preferably be *What* orientated as already indicated. This keeps the Driver's mind focused upon the big picture and results orientated which is their organising priority. Similarly with facts, show them probabilities of success or the effectiveness of the various options they may have in buying your product. Again, the Driver wants to know what *they* will achieve in buying your product. A golden rule with Driver customers is, then, to never state a fact without at the same time stating its benefit. For example, "[state the fact] ... *What this means to you is* [state the benefit]...". This again keeps their mind focused on the bottom line outcome.

Should disagreement arise over facts then again stick to the facts and do not try to win the Driver over with personal assurances or charm. Where agreement is reached support the facts not the person. More importantly temper your impulse for self-promotion. While your natural enthusiasm will be appreciated it can make some Expressives prone to rely upon personality and this will alienate the Driver who will feel they are being forced to succumb to your will - their basic fear.

Avoid speculating or offering other than exactly what you know can be delivered in terms of performance, this means backing your enthusiasm with facts. As regards testimonials, the Driver will probably not to very interested in them and will if necessary delegate these and other minor details to a subordinate.

*Response guide to questions*

The Driver wants you to get to the point quickly and does not want long-winded answers to their questions, 'Yes' and 'No' answers are often sufficient. They want you to be business-like, efficient and brief. Stick to the main features of your product or bottom-line results. Speak with confidence and authority.

*Questions to ask*
- How do you feel you can best achieve your objectives?
- *What* have you done about them so far?
- Which option do you believe best achieves your objective?
- Is this agreed?
- When do you want it by?

*Areas to avoid*

Do not be indecisive when dealing with this type of person, they want you to provide them with answers, not problems. Inefficiency is not looked upon favourably so do what you say you will, or do not offer at all. Do not bore them with details take care of them yourself whenever possible.

*Closing the Sale*

One thing that characterises a Driver is their ability to make quick decisions, so expect one at the end of your presentation. To avoid an outright verbal rejection, which this personality type has no qualms in giving, facilitate the decision making process by asking for a decision in the form of an alternative close. This leaves the final decision with them but at the same time appeals to their instinct for self-reliance. If you are seen to vacillate at the point of sale the Driver will seize the initiative and reject your proposal outright.

Having concluded business with the Driver make a gracious, but nonetheless speedy, exit. The Driver really will not appreciate your lingering to chat informally.

*Organising priorities*

You are inclined to adopt a selling style based upon the following priorities: The *Who-Why-What-How*. To sell to the Driver customer you need to re-arrange you priorities in the following sequence: The *What-How-Who-Why*. They are results orientated individuals who are not concerned with relationships in that they don't need to like you to buy from you. Your selling style therefore needs to be focused on their basic desire for self-reliance.

**Snapshot Profile**
- You have a *Who* selling style. The Driver customer has a *What* buying style (see diagram 8)
- The Driver's *Basic Desire* - Self-reliance
- The Driver's *Basic Fear* - Submitting to the will of others (see diagram 9)

## Selling to Amiable customers

As both you and the Amiable are characterised by your genuine concern for others you will relate well. In this regard your respective basic desires are relationship orientated. The Amiable will find you warm, personable and stimulating. This is a good foundation upon which to build and, provided you can sustain this approach throughout the presentation, there is an increased likelihood they will buy from you. However, sustaining this approach may prove challenging. Being valued is more important to the Amiable than 'merely' being accepted (see diagram 9). To meet the Amiable's basic desire to feel needed you will need to modify your selling style by spending time establishing a their trust. Consequently caution is needed to ensure your initial excellent first impression does not turn to dust. The warm reception you will get from an Amiable is in many ways a danger area as some Expressives will seize upon the opportunity to talk about them. While this may appeal to your basic desire to be accepted it is sure to alienate the Amiable who wants to talk about their needs and desires.

*The Sales Presentation*
Patience should be your watchword when dealing with all Amiables so it is particularly important that the Expressive salesperson modifies their selling style to take account of this. Your patience will be required to establish what the Amiable's objectives are, and again when showing *Why* your product will help them achieve those objectives. The Amiable needs to have a reason *Why* they should buy your product and in the absence of a good reason there is little chance of them buying. So give the Amiable a reason to buy from you, other than the fact that you are the seller. It is important therefore that you take the time to uncover the Amiable customer's underlying motivation. This is of course their basic desire to feel needed or valued as a person.

While the genuine enthusiasm you exude will be appreciated by the Amiable it is necessary your temper your approach slightly as some Amiable customers will interpret your enthusiasm as being 'loud' and 'pushy'. It is worth remembering that Amiables are quiet and reserved individuals who like to get to know and trust people gradually. Any sign of intolerance or boredom on your part will be counter-productive as without their trust it is unlikely they will buy from you. Moreover, perceived intolerance or boredom is likely to appeal to their basic fear of being unneeded, or under-valued.

Your characteristic lack of attention to the fine details may also alienate the Amiable. You will therefore need to modify your selling style to include as many details and facts about you product as possible. You should also be prepared to deliver this information in a slow and measured manner. Any approach not measured will ultimately be futile because the Amiable is likely to simply 'switch-off'.

In contrast to the Amiable customer's more 'inhibited' style your body language may be rather too animated for some. Such 'loud' actions can be intimidating to the Amiable so you need to be more restrained than you might otherwise be when selling. Another potential problem area is the Expressive's talent for quick thinking. They like to generate ideas by the dozen and throw them around like confetti. However this cuts little sway with the Amiable who prefers to take ideas one at a time. Be prepared to introduce ideas in a logical manner and avoiding 'off-the-wall' ideas because the Amiable prefers the tried and tested solution.

While you are inclined to be impulsive the Amiable is cautious in nature and so has an aversion to risk. They will certainly not buy on impulse as they need to know the facts and understand the implications involved. It is important therefore that you take the time to go through these facts until the Amiable is completely satisfied. Dealing with facts and figure with this type of customer is though less daunting from your point of view than you might think. Indeed they are nothing like as detail orientated as the Analytical customer, but Amiables are nonetheless cautious individuals. Having said this the Amiable, unlike the Analytical, will accept personal assurances, providing of course you have built up trust with them. Where disagreement arises over the facts be careful not to hurt the Amiable customer's feelings. Disagreements if not handled carefully can appeal to their basic fear. When you have agreement be sure to move casually and informally on to the next point. Do not rush or jolly them along.

If you have at your disposal a range of possible solutions to the Amiable's problem then it will pay dividends, as with the Analytical, to focus upon the tried and tested. If your product has certain guarantees with it then offer them, or at the very least offer them assurance that their decision will minimise risk. Do not offer more than you can actually deliver as failure will be taken as a betrayal of trust. You should also be prepared to put in writing any assurances you do give and failure to agree to this will arouse their suspicions, justified or not.

Your modified selling style should be of the soft and non-threatening variety with emphasis upon the tried and tested over the innovative, and this is also the case when closing the sale.

*Response guide to questions*
The Amiable personality likes things to be taken slowly and wants to be sure that you are trustworthy. Answer their questions fully, while at the same time demonstrating that you genuinely care about them. Provide proof of your answers whenever possible. Speak in a slow non-threatening manner.

*Questions to ask*
- *Why* do you feel that way?
- *Why* is that important to you?
- Do you feel this is the right thing to do?
- Do you feel we can work together on this?
- Can you see *why* this is the right course of action?

*Areas to avoid*
Avoid rushing or cajoling the Amiable customer. Show patience and tolerance and in this way earn their trust and confidence in you. Be firm and friendly, but not insensitive to their feelings.

*Closing the Sale*
Cajoling at the point of sale, or using gimmicks, will undermine everything that has gone before. But then neither should leave the decision to them as the Amiable customer is unlikely to be responded to with a firm decision either way. A measured close is much more likely to receive a favourable reception. As with the body of your sales presentation any closing statement or question needs to place emphasis on the personal benefits they will gain. For example, *"Can you see why this is the right decision for you?"* Alternatively, *"I am confident that these proposals meet your needs"*. But no matter how well prepared you are, be prepared for them to procrastinate and be ready to restate the

benefits in the form of a close. You may even need to make a second visit to see an Amiable to 'demonstrate' or prove to them that they are valued.

*Organising priorities*

You are inclined to adopt a selling style based upon the following priorities: The *Who-Why-What-How*. To sell to the Amiable customer you need to re-arrange you priorities in the following sequence: The *Why-Who-How-What*. This is still a selling process based upon emotion but one where the emphasis needs to shift from your desire to be accepted toward their desire to be valued.

**Snapshot Profile**

- You have a *Who* selling style. The Amiable customer has a *Why* buying style (see diagram 8)
- The Amiable's *Basic Desire* - To be loved, needed, or valued
- The Amiable's *Basic Fear* - Being unloved, unneeded or under-valued (see diagram 9)

## Selling to fellow Expressive customers

When two Expressive personalities meet there is usually instant rapport. Your outgoing friendly greeting will be reciprocated with an equally warm reception from the Expressive customer. The incorporation of innovative ideas inherent in your selling style will also hit fertile ground and be responded to with equally creative ones from the customer. There will of course be no need for you to adjust the tempo of your selling style to match the buying style of the Expressive customer. You can let rip with full gusto sure of a receptive audience with this type of customer. As regards the details and facts and figures - the minimum you use the better. Take a few of your favourite testimonials along too, what works for you will work for this customer.

Immersed in this 'ideal' environment you might imagine that no guidance is needed when meeting such a warm and receptive customer. But caution is needed for underlying all such encounters are subtle motivations which might turn this 'ideal' encounter into a lose/lose outcome. For while you both desire acceptance and fear rejection, you might achieve you desire at the expense of them feeling rejected. It is therefore important that selling style be modified to shift the emphasis from your desires to the customers (see diagram 9).

*The Sales Presentation*

As in any sales situation differing motivations come into play with both the salesperson and the customer attempting to satisfy their basic desires and avoid their basic fears. This does not change simply because two individuals with the same desires and fears meet. It is therefore important we examine possible consequences arising from such situations. In particular, contrast the dangers of attempting to appeal solely to your own desires with that of the benefits of transcending the impulse.

Given that you are both status orientated individuals it is important that you do not try to 'out do' you customer. You should never imply you drive a better car, take better holidays, live in a bigger house, or know more influential people when selling to fellow Expressives. Even if you can 'out do' them in these areas it will not endear you to the Expressive customer - more likely you'll make them feel inferior and thus rejected. This impulse, if not resisted, would also reveal your true concern of self-interest making any claims to show an interest in others disingenuous. Indeed, in 'winning' you will merely have succeeded in appealing to the Expressive customer's basic fears. Clearly such a 'contest' will result in lose/lose outcome. In resisting any such impulse of course the reverse applies in that the Expressive customer feels good about themselves and their achievements, and so feels accepted. This modified approach in your selling style not only shows more genuine concern for others but it is more likely to succeed in producing the outcome you desire.

The process of disintegration described above does not of course imply that all Expressive personalities are narcissistic and pretentious, only that it is a characteristic vice. Like all vices it need never be made manifest in your behaviour but if, on honest reflection, you have this tendency it can be overcome by modifying your selling style to one that places emphasis on the interests of others, not yourself.

On the other hand, even if the Expressive customer feels the impulse to demonstrate their higher social standing, greater income, and the like then let them do so, you must always resist it. Support them, praise them or acknowledge them as appropriate. In 'rising to the bait' there is the inherent danger that you will become chameleon-like by doing and saying whatever is felt will project the right image to the customer. Not 'rising to the bait' is, as I have indicated, is conducive to win/win outcomes. This is because a quiet self-acceptance, or acknowledgement of your limitations, makes you inwardly rather than outwardly directed. Fortified by this self-acceptance your concern, or commitment, becomes directed toward the customer, and not supportive of your image. Paradoxically in pursuing this line you will find more to value within yourself than you do in status symbols, or the public's perception of you.

In having avoided this major error, which is a common occurrence when two Expressives meet in a competitive environment, you will be able to exercise the discipline necessary to ensure all the creativity interjected into your sales presentation results in a win/win conclusion rather than nothing. Your emphasis during your sales presentation must, then, be directed to your customer's basic desire for acceptance.

Though much of what you do naturally will find favour with the fellow Expressive the guides below might prove useful.

*Response guide to questions*
The Expressive customer often prefers to socialise than talk business. Their questions often reflect a personal desire to be friendly - so reciprocate. Keep factual answers regarding the product simple, if you can get away with a 'Yes' or 'No' answer then do so. They are not overly concerned with proof, or facts and figures so keep them to a bare minimum covering only the high points. Speak with enthusiasm and become animated too.

*Questions to ask*
- Am I right in assuming you will make the final decision?
- Your colleagues will feel the same way I'm sure, don't you agree?

- Based upon your knowledge of the subject which solution do you feel works best?
- I feel I can work with you on this, how do you feel about me?
- Shall I take care of all the necessary paperwork for you?

*Areas to avoid*

Do not allow this type of customer to distract you from the true purpose of your meeting by talking too much. Do not bore them with procedure - just take care of it.

*Closing the Sale*

It is a typical outcome of a sales presentation involving two Expressive individuals to leave the decision to buy hanging. Therefore closing the sale requires you to take the initiative. Often the simplest way to take the initiative is to offer an alternative close. For example *"I can see you are a decisive person so which option should we go for ...?"* Expressive customers, like you, will want to get business out of the way quickly and, provided they like you, will often buy with the shortest of presentations.

*Organising priorities*

You are inclined to adopt a selling style, and the Expressive customer inclined to adopt a buying style, based upon the following priorities: The *Who-Why-What-How*. To sell to the fellow Expressive customer requires no change in emphasis merely a re-direction of your attention away from you and toward them.

**Snapshot Profile**
- You have a *Who* selling style. The Expressive customer has a *Who* buying style (see diagram 8)
- The Expressive's *Basic Desire* - To be accepted
- The Expressive's *Basic Fear* - Being rejected (see diagram 9)

# 13 - Concluding comments

## Qualities & Skills

Over time the circumstances under which we must operate changes, but people seldom do. Therefore, what you have learnt about how different customers buy will remain largely immutable. These new skills are not of course all that is required to achieve sales success. A professional salesperson must possess some personal qualities and other skills if they are to meet the challenges of an increasingly competitive market place, and thrive. We cannot achieve above average performance with average qualities and skills! These personal qualities and additional skills can be summarised as follows:

## Qualities

*Versatility*

A capacity to adapt in various situations. A willingness to consider other ways of tackling a problem. A many-sided approach to selling.

*Understanding*

A sympathetic perception of others. To recognise and appreciate the different desires and fears that motivate a customer.

*Respect*

To pay attention and give consideration to the needs, status and opinions of customers.

*Patience*

The capacity to endure difficulties with calmness and composure. The quality of being prepared to wait without rage or frustration.

*Integrity*

An incorruptible character in relation to fair dealing, uprightness, honesty and sincerity.

*Honesty*

The quality of decency, truthfulness, openness and fair-dealing with customers.

*Resolve*

Firmness or steadfastness of purpose. A resolution to complete what has been started.

*Decisiveness*

The capacity to make clear and unequivocal decisions when required.

# Skills

*Communication*

The ability to impart or convey ideas, knowledge and information, whether verbally or non-verbally, in a way customers can readily understand.

*Interpersonal sensitivity*

A conscious awareness of the impact we have on customers and the capacity to modify our selling style accordingly to avoid alienating them.

*Listening*

The art of attentive hearing. To pay attention to, and understand, what the customer is saying, whether we agree with them or not.

*Perception*

The intuitive recognition or understanding of a situation, and the ability to accurately grasp the implications.

*Control over personal prejudice/biases*

The ability to avoid habitual generalisations that impose beliefs, attributes, defects or qualities upon customers which they do not actually possess.

*Foresight*

The faculty of foreseeing the inevitable or probable consequences of a given action.

*Mediation*

The capacity to transact as an intermediary between our needs and the needs of the customer.

Each of these qualities and skills are essential if we are to sell in a manner enabling us to satisfy our own substantive interests and preserve the relationship with the customer. In other words, to achieve win/win outcomes. What has been outlined to you in these pages is consistent with each of these qualities and skills.

## Taking action

It is often assumed that knowledge is intelligence, but knowledge is at best only enlightenment and at worst information, neither of which guarantee action. Intelligence in contrast is a way of acting. And as Huxley wrote; *'The great end of life is not knowledge but action'* So whatever knowledge or information we have it must function as an intellectual skill in the sales process. Knowledge that does not serve this function offers its possessor nothing but promise.

Those factors that might prevent an individual from taking action are either one, or a combination of, the following: self-doubt, reluctance to change, procrastination, overwhelming problems, an unrealistic view of life. Transcending these is crucial if the information gleaned from this modest book is to be of any practical benefit. Given the potential obstacles a few words about each to close this book might therefore be helpful.

*Self-doubt*

We can never be certain of life's outcomes. However, we can be certain that there is no future in doing no wrong. To assume that in making no mistakes we will succeed is folly - the person who makes no mistakes usually makes nothing. We all experience doubt from time-to-time but we must never permit doubt to prevent us from ever attempting. Our doubts are traitors to the good we might achieve. And while we can all, and often do, rationalise our doubts they are in the main based upon insecurities rather than reality. This emotional diet can never be satiated, its deficiency is necessary for its survival.

*Reluctance to change*

Nothing is certain but uncertainty itself and the absurd person is one who never changes. One of the great gifts of life of is that there is no limit or quota on our possibilities, whether imposed or chosen. Surely it is better to determine, where we can, those possibilities and in doing so control the direction of inevitable change. Let us not forget either that change is acceptable to us if we know its direction. So it is goals we must pursue.

*Procrastination*

Procrastination is opportunities natural assassin. The doer, to achieve, must be up and doing. Make a decision, act and continue to act. It is surely better to be worn-out with action than rust away through inaction.

*Overwhelming Problems*

Problems are to life what carbon is to steel. They are both desirable and necessary; life without problems would hardly be worth living, and the only problem free life is called death. This does not prevent us from experiencing the feeling of being overwhelmed by problems of course. To overcome them requires you to determine your path and act - solutions 1,2 & 3 above.

*An unrealistic view of life*

Life is neither fair nor just and to get we must give. In short, we must show enough people how to get what they want before we can get what we want. Therefore, we need to be life's 'go givers' rather than 'go-getters'. Complaining about life's misfortunes makes us disputable, hesitant, dilatory and irresolute. In any of these we confine ourselves in a life destined to experience disenchantment, frustration and regret - a wholly unsatisfactory place of self-consignment when you think about it!

Steve Deery 2013

www.ingramcontent.com/pod-product-compliance
Lightning Source LLC
LaVergne TN
LVHW020210150125
801329LV00007B/261